The Shakespeare Handbooks

WITHDRAWN

THE SHAKESPEARE HANDBOOKS

Series Editor: John Russell Brown

PUBLISHED

FORTHCOMING

The Shakespeare Handbooks

Julius Caesar

David Carnegie

palgrave
macmillan

First published 2009 by
PALGRAVE MACMILLAN

Palgrave Macmillan in the UK is an imprint of Macmillan Publishers Limited, registered in England, company number 785998, of Houndmills, Basingstoke, Hampshire RG21 6XS.

Palgrave Macmillan in the US is a division of St Martin's Press LLC, 175 Fifth Avenue, New York, NY 10010.

Palgrave Macmillan is the global academic imprint of the above companies and has companies and representatives throughout the world.

Palgrave® and Macmillan® are registered trademarks in the United States, the United Kingdom, Europe and other countries

ISBN-13: 978-1-4039-4890-8   hardback
ISBN-10: 1-4039-4890-9   hardback
ISBN-13: 978-1-4039-4891-5   paperback
ISBN-10: 1-4039-4891-7   paperback

This book is printed on paper suitable for recycling and made from fully managed and sustained forest sources. Logging, pulping and manufacturing processes are expected to conform to the environmental regulations of the country of origin.

A catalogue record for this book is available from the British Library.

A catalog record for this book is available from the Library of Congress.

10   9   8   7   6   5   4   3   2   1
18 17 16 15 14 13 12 11 10 09

Printed and bound in China

Contents

General Editor's Preface

The Shakespeare Handbooks provide an innovative way of studying the plays in performance. The commentaries, which are their core feature, enable a reader to envisage the words of a text unfurling in performance, involving actions and meanings not readily perceived except in rehearsal or performance. The aim is to present the plays in the environment for which they were written and to offer an experience as close as possible to an audience's progressive experience of a production.

While each book has the same range of contents, their authors have been encouraged to shape them according to their own critical and scholarly understanding and their first-hand experience of theatre practice. The various chapters are designed to complement the commentaries: the cultural context of each play is presented together with quotations from original sources; the authority of its text or texts is considered with what is known of the earliest performances; key performances and productions of its subsequent stage history are both described and compared. The aim in all this has been to help readers to develop their own informed and imaginative view of a play in ways that supplement the provision of standard editions and are more user-friendly than detailed stage histories or collections of criticism from diverse sources.

Further volumes are in preparation so that, within a few years, the Shakespeare Handbooks will be available for all the plays that are frequently performed and studied.

John Russell Brown

Preface

I was lucky, I think, to first experience professional Shakespeare at the vast, open, thrust stage of the Stratford Festival in Canada. Although I have seen many other productions (and films) of *Julius Caesar* since then, I have never lost that early discovery that the essentials of this and all Shakespeare's plays are simply actors and an audience in a shared space – bodies and words in action on a bare stage.

To write about a Shakespeare play is to relive those earlier productions, but it is also to call on every available resource of both scholarship and the theatre. I am indebted to all the writers whom I quote, and many more besides, whose research has helped form such knowledge, critical thinking, and judgement as I can claim. In addition, I am grateful to the many actors, directors, designers, technicians, and dramaturgs whom I have worked with and learned from. Bringing together the all-too-often-separate worlds of the university and the working theatre is productive indeed for the understanding of Shakespeare.

It is a pleasure to acknowledge a few more specific debts. First, to Phil Mann, colleague and friend, from whom I have learned an immense amount about the difficult business of simplicity in conveying emotion and meaning on stage. I worked as dramaturg with him on his professional production of *Julius Caesar* for Circa Theatre, Wellington in 1999, and more recently he directed my students in a thorough deconstruction of the play in performance. To all my students over the years, and especially those who took part in *Julius Caesar*, and in John Webster's Roman tragedy *Appius and Virginia*, I am also grateful. Among many academic colleagues I owe particular debts to David Gunby and Mac Jackson, who co-edited *Appius and Virginia* with me, to Geoff Miles and Matthew Trundle for their deep classical knowledge, and to David O'Donnell and Matt Wagner and other theatre colleagues for their Shakespearean knowledge and generous support.

Julie McDougall and David Lawrence provided invaluable research assistance.

Among many libraries and theatre archives I owe special thanks to the Billy Rose Theatre Collection at the New York Public Library, and to the Hampden-Booth Theatre Library at the Players, also in New York; to the Folger Shakespeare Library in Washington; to the Shakespeare Centre in Stratford and the Theatre Museum and Shakespeare Globe Centre in London; and to the Alexander Turnbull Library of the National Library of New Zealand in Wellington. I am grateful to Michael Billington for a long and illuminating talk about *Julius Caesar*, and to all the other theatre critics whose record of Shakespearean performances is so vital to a work like this. In addition, Kate Wallis, Sonya Barker, and the other staff at Palgrave Macmillan have been unfailingly supportive through the sadly protracted period of writing this book.

A final thank you must go to two outstanding scholars to whom I owe my passion for Shakespeare in performance: to Brian Parker, whose teaching first inspired me and whose subsequent mentoring and friendship has been a constant support and pleasure; and to John Russell Brown, another lifelong friend and mentor. As general editor of this series he continues to provide inspiration and encouragement for which I am deeply grateful.

To my late wife Pauline, who was both the sternest and the most constructive critic of all my writing, this book, of necessity completed without her help, is dedicated.

1 The Text and Early Performances

Stoop, then, and wash. How many ages hence
Shall this our lofty scene be acted over
In states unborn and accents yet unknown!

(III.i.111–13)

This response by Cassius to Brutus' injunction to 'bathe our hands in Caesar's blood / Up to the elbows' (ll. 106–7) is remarkable in its invitation to the audience to respond not just to the death of Julius Caesar seconds earlier, and to the deliberate glorification of the assassination by the conspirators, but also to the self-conscious theatricality of an actor invoking an image of future actors re-staging the scene for centuries to come to other audiences in other countries and languages. We are invited to respond emotionally, even viscerally, to the bloody moment, but at the same time to admire the intellectual double focus: Shakespeare, through Cassius, is using his own craft of the theatre (the 'lofty scene') to point out the momentous reverberations of an action that is as true when re-staged as when first performed. For actors to draw audience attention to the fact that it is only a play requires audacity; to do so in a way that deepens our response to the play is masterful.

However, the lines quoted above tell us less than we could wish to know about how Shakespeare's company, the Lord Chamberlain's Men, staged this moment. Did Cassius remain standing and speaking while the other conspirators stooped around the body of Caesar? If so, did his words seem to be a form of commentary to the audience, perhaps legitimizing what might otherwise appear brutal, even psychotic? Or did Cassius stoop and smear his own arms before 'How many ages hence'? Would that acting decision be more likely to make his own bloody appearance undercut the claim to noble action? Are the rest of the conspirators confident in their bloody arms and swords as emblems of liberty for Rome; or do they exhibit uncertainty at the spectacle, perhaps starting to fear that they have left Caesar 'a carcass fit for hounds' rather than 'a dish fit for the gods' (II.i.174–5)? And whatever they think of themselves, what is the audience drawn to think? These questions and more face the actors (and in modern theatre, the directors, designers and others) in every new production of the play. The text of the play is first and foremost a story in potential, waiting to be given life in performance with the willing collaboration of spectators.

We are fortunate to have an eyewitness account from one of the early spectators of *Julius Caesar* at the new Globe Theatre (then only recently erected on the south bank of the Thames from the timbers of the company's old theatre, surreptitiously removed from its previous site in the north of London). Thomas Platter, a Swiss doctor, was a tourist in London in the autumn of 1599, and recounts that:

> On the 21st of September, after dinner, at about two o'clock, I went with my party across the water; in the straw-thatched house we saw the tragedy of the first Emperor Julius Caesar, very pleasingly performed, with approximately fifteen characters; at the end of the play they danced together admirably and exceedingly gracefully, according to their custom, two in each group dressed in men's and two in women's apparel.
>
> (Humphreys, p. 1)

Quite apart from Platter's pleasure at the Elizabethan theatre custom of finishing a play with a jig, it is clear that he enjoyed and responded to the drama itself. Nor did he have any doubt that it was 'the tragedy of . . . Julius Caesar'. He took particular note of the 'approximately fifteen characters', which appears an odd reaction to a play with over fifty parts; it seems likely he meant 'fifteen actors'. There are fourteen or sixteen or so characters on stage in the busiest scene, III.i (the exact number depends on whether there are non-speaking senators, lictors, guards, etc.), which presumably explains Platter's statement. Since the Lord Chamberlain's Men at this time probably had ten or so principal actors, and maybe six hired men to play minor roles and groups such as commoners, senators, or soldiers, plus youths to play the female roles and pages such as Lucius, most of the company was on stage in the early part of III.i.

What is surprising is that Shakespeare wrote so many more roles than he had actors. Given more than fifty identifiable roles in the play, nearly all the actors except those playing Brutus, Cassius, and Mark Antony (and perhaps Caesar) would have had to double at least one other role, and some several. While Shakespeare was familiar from his English history plays with how to write his scenes to allow time backstage for doubling, in *Julius Caesar* he was under less historical compulsion to do so. A number of the conspirators with Brutus when Caesar was assassinated were also with him to the end, and present at the battle of Philippi. Why, then, did Shakespeare in effect kill off all the conspirators except Brutus and Cassius at the end of III.i? Why not retain Casca, Decius, Metellus Cimber, Trebonius and the rest, rather than presenting the audience in Act IV with Lucilius, Titinius, Messala and many other new characters? It is a striking theatrical decision that reinforces the sense of readers and directors that the play is divided in two, and it tends to support a critical view that whereas Shakespeare was intent on portraying in the first half a critical action in the history of the world, he had more interest in the second half in exploring the personal and emotional repercussions of the act, and perhaps in ensuring sympathy for Brutus (see pp. 145–6).

Platter also took note of the 'straw-thatched' playhouse (its new thatch conspicuous on Bankside). It is virtually certain that *Julius Caesar* was one of the first plays performed at the new Globe, perhaps the first. Shakespeare knew the kind of theatre he was writing for, and that he, as an actor in the Lord Chamberlain's Men, would perform in. Visual spectacle, such as the tableau of the conspirators holding aloft their bloody swords, was an essential element of his stagecraft, a central part of telling a story on a large, bare platform stage with almost nothing of what we would call scenery. The stage was architecture for the actor, not a realist scenic environment within which the fictional characters lived. It was the actors who provided nearly all the spectacle which worked in tandem with their words to inform the spectators where they should imagine the story to be.

The stage doors – certainly one at each end of the tiring-house façade behind the actors; and probably a large central opening, perhaps reserved for spectacular entries such as Caesar's in I.ii – did not in themselves resemble any particular door, but any door that might be needed. Indeed, although Flavius and Marullus enter at the start of the play from one door, and encounter the commoners entering from the door at the other side, we quickly forget the doors and accept, from the dialogue, that the scene takes place in a public street. The doors, in other words, belong to the theatre, not to scenic fiction. The effect is so simple, however, that it is easy to miss how powerfully it points to the essence of the entire scene: what matters is not architecture or scenery, but the fact that the scene is an encounter, a confrontation of energies from different directions. The same effect is used at I.iii.0.1 when Casca meets Cicero, and when the armies parley in Acts IV and V. Similarly, for characters to leave by different doors, as Marullus and Flavius do at the end of the first scene, and Portia and Lucius at the end of III.i, is a simple and powerful image of independent action by each. By contrast, characters entering or leaving together give a strong image of association, whether of friendship or purpose (the entry of Marullus and Flavius together, even prior to confronting the commoners, illustrates the point).

The entry of large processions, perhaps by the impressive central opening, provides meaningful spectacle in itself: the first time we see Caesar he carries with him a train of followers like a comet's tail. The power and importance of the greatest man in the world is emphasized by the size of the procession, and its purposeful direction across the stage and out after the interruption by the Soothsayer. And the stage, having been full of people a moment earlier – at least twelve actors – suddenly becomes quiet with just two men left: Cassius and Brutus. Naturally, our attention and interest are drawn to them; later, when the procession returns, these two men remain of special interest, because we have seen them apart from the procession.

Whether we are focused on one or two characters, or on a stage full of people, whether we think of the Globe performances or modern productions, costume plays a vital part in our understanding. On the bare Elizabethan stage the actors' costume was even more important than in a modern production, because costume was almost the only visual display available, and also because Elizabethan sumptuary laws laid down by statute who could wear what materials in everyday life (commoners had to wear hats of wool, and were forbidden to wear the velvet, satin, silk, or other rich materials that knights could; cloth-of-gold was reserved to the aristocracy; and so on). When Flavius and Marullus berate the commoners for their dress in I.i, they do so in precise terms. Profession, social standing, and wealth were minutely indicated by clothing, and audiences could recognize the code.

How this code worked for a play set in Roman times is difficult to determine, because we do not know how historicized the costume was. The three main possibilities are that costume was contemporary, that it was Roman, or that it was a mixture of the two. In support of the argument that such plays would have been performed in contemporary costume, critics point to a number of Elizabethan references in *Julius Caesar*: Casca's toga with a 'sleeve' to be plucked (I.ii.179), Caesar's 'doublet' (I.ii.263) and 'nightgown' (II.ii.o.2), the conspirators' 'hats' and 'cloaks' (II.i.73–4), Brutus walking 'unbracèd' (II.i.263), and wearing a 'gown' with a 'pocket' (IV.ii.303). Other Roman plays of the period include references to 'Renaissance accessories: silk stockings, ladies' masks and cork-soled shoes, rebatoes, billements (spangled headtires) and similar finery' (MacIntyre, pp. 258–9). Given also chiming clocks and other non-Roman elements, this is a basis for claiming that Shakespeare constructed his Roman society in terms of their Elizabethan equivalents, that audiences at the time would read the visual codes accordingly, and that we therefore must be alert to these codes.

An alternative view is that Roman costume was used (or at least, Roman as the Renaissance understood its costuming). Part of this argument is based on the fact that Elizabethan words might be used to translate Latin words for Roman garments (like 'gown' for 'toga'; the reference to Caesar's 'doublet' mentioned above is actually taken from North's translation of Plutarch), and part on contemporary designs and inventories of 'antique' costumes such as shaped breastplates, plumed helmets, and senators' togas (see Humphreys, pp. 50–1 and Ronan, pp. 76–9).

A third possibility is that there was a 'mixed' style. The famous 'Peacham drawing' (reproduced by Humphreys, p. 50) appears to depict a scene from Shakespeare's *Titus Andronicus* with the major male characters wearing an approximation of Roman dress, but other characters and soldiers wearing Elizabethan dress. In some cases characters may have worn a suggestion of Roman costume over Elizabethan clothing. In that case, the Roman costume elements become emblematic and representative of historical period and individual status rather than realistic depiction.

The appearance of the senators may serve to illustrate how costume affects meaning. Many references from plays of the period confirm that senators on stage normally wore scarlet gowns. (Historically Roman senators had only a band of 'purpura' bordering their white togas, but Renaissance authorities seem to have understood the gowns of the senate to have been entirely the colour of 'purple blood'.) If the costuming was Elizabethan, then the stage image of the senate would be of an assembly of scarlet-gowned judges. Caesar seated on a raised throne in the Capitol (III.i) might well have looked, to a London audience, like a monarch surrounded by his judges or nobility. And since all the men would be in doublet and hose, the distinction between senators and soldiers would not be great, apart from the gowns. (Stage soldiers often wore the crescent-shaped 'gorget', throat armour, to represent full armour.) However, in either a Roman or a 'mixed' style, the scarlet togas of the senate would have presented a picture not of a hierarchical monarchy, but of the Roman Republic. The implications of the death of a potential king would be very different.

Large properties would also have had a role to play in creating spectacle and influencing audience interpretation. Just as a recognizable stage throne on a dais might imply royal legitimacy for Caesar, so special benches for the senators might invoke historical knowledge of the Roman senate. (*Julius Caesar* does not absolutely require such seating, but some other Roman plays of the period did specify them.) When Brutus describes the dead Caesar as lying 'on Pompey's basis', does that mean that a statue of Pompey with a base on which Caesar could fall, as described in Plutarch's history (see p. 104), was provided on stage? Or is Brutus simply painting a word picture? Or does the dais, the 'basis', for the throne substitute imaginatively for the basis for a statue? We do not know, any more than we know how Brutus' tent was indicated in Act IV. But our lack of knowledge does not mean the questions are unimportant, for visual signs help orient an audience in its reception of the play's emotion and meaning.

Small props serve the same function, and often have a symbolic as well as a pragmatic function. For instance, any book on stage is likely to signal melancholy (as in *Hamlet*, for instance), so Brutus' reading is an indication of more than a desire to sleep. A sword may stand for 'Justice', as in some of Queen Elizabeth's famous portraits, so the manner in which the swords are held during the assassination scene may be significant. Even stage blood is important, since both savage blood-letting and noble suicide were widely regarded as particularly Roman attributes.

The trumpets and drums which contribute much of the sense of battle on the Elizabethan stage are only part of a Roman context of trumpet flourishes and 'sennets' frequently specified in the stage directions. Lucius' lute is the only relief from the harshness of Roman public music. '*Thunder and lightning*' are called for at the start of both I.iii and II.ii, as if 'The heavens themselves blaze forth the death of princes' (II. ii.31). The thunder continues throughout I.iii (note the stage direction '*Thunder still*' at l. 100), Shakespeare's first use of this effect (which would develop further in *Macbeth*) to reinforce the mood of an entire scene. It may also have been the first significant use of the new thunder machine at the Globe. Does the thunder continue ominously in the background of the orchard scene (II.i), as in some modern productions, or does the brief stage direction 'Thunder' at the last line of the scene merely prepare for its resumption in II.ii? How will each choice affect an audience as it views the conspirators?

We are often faced with questions like these that underline how little we know about the original productions. Even hints, therefore, are valuable. The author of one of the commendatory poems prefaced to the Shakespeare First Folio in 1623, Leonard Digges, declared that he could not and would not believe Shakespeare dead until some other playwright could match *Romeo and Juliet*,

> Or till I hear a scene more nobly take
> Than when thy half-sword parleying Romans spake.

That this refers to the quarrel scene between Brutus and Cassius, IV.ii, is confirmed by a later version of Digges's poem. Since *Julius Caesar* was not published prior to 1623, the comment must refer to contemporary staging. It may be surprising to think of both men having their swords half-drawn in their anger – and some eighteenth-century productions lost any sense of subtlety by having the two repeatedly clash their sword hilts together – but it is a useful reminder of how the energy of actors makes this one of the most memorable scenes in the play.

Ben Jonson, Shakespeare's contemporary, found the play memorable for a different reason. Despite his admiration for Shakespeare, he joked at the absurdity of Caesar replying to Metellus that 'Caesar did never wrong, but with just cause', and Jonson even put the line in one of his plays as a joke. It would seem to make sense as a joke in a play only if audiences had heard it in *Julius Caesar*. However, Caesar does not say this in the text as we have it (III.i.47–8). This leads us from the first performances to consideration of the First Folio.

The First Folio

The first actors of *The Tragedy of Julius Caesar* (as it is called in the First Folio) did not have a printed book from which to learn their parts or study the play; they had only handwritten copies of their own parts, with the skimpiest of cues indicating when to speak. There would have been a complete manuscript copy of the play that had been authorized by the Master of the Revels, the 'Book' that was the company's licence to perform, but that is long lost. The only authoritative text of the entire play that survives is that in the First Folio of 1623, the collected edition of Shakespeare's works published seven years after his death.

Whereas writing is a solitary activity, producing and publishing plays are communal activities with many social interactions and collaborations involved. A scribe wrote out the parts for the actors, and errors were possible. Changes might be introduced during the brief rehearsal period (especially when one of the actors, Shakespeare, was also the playwright), or during subsequent performances of the play, for a variety of reasons. Any confusions in the text could be resolved, the book-keeper (what we would call stage manager or prompter) might adjust a scene to fit the company's resources, actors might invent new lines or cut unsatisfactory ones, depending on audience reaction, or the playwright himself might revise the play.

A similar range of interaction applied when a play was published. Shakespeare would initially have written the play out himself, but there may have been scratchings-out, insertions, and even minor confusions, as is common in most authors' drafts. A scribe probably copied the entire play into a fair copy, and it was probably such a fair copy that was given to the printers in 1623. But revisions by Shakespeare or others could have been added to that fair copy beforehand. Then the compositors in the printing house added their contribution: adopting their own favourite spellings, inserting punctuation they thought was needed (for punctuation was at this period much more the responsibility of the actor in the theatre or the compositor in the printing house than of the author). Compositors might also misread their manuscript copy, whether because it was badly written, or because they were tired, lazy, or even drunk. Thus, given the collaborative nature of both theatre and publishing, and the continuing performance and possibly adjustment of the play, we can have no certainty about how close the 1623 First Folio text is to what was first performed in 1599, or to how Shakespeare wished it to be performed when he finally retired from the company.

That Jonson laughed at a line that does not appear in the Folio suggests the possibility that Shakespeare realized that he had written an absurdity, and changed the line to what we have: 'Know, Caesar doth not wrong, nor without cause / Will he be satisfied' (III.i.47–8). But it is not enough in itself to prove the case (though the Oxford *Complete Works/Norton Shakespeare* has accepted Jonson's evidence as to what

Shakespeare originally wrote, and reads 'Know Caesar doth not wrong but with just cause, / Nor without cause will he be satisfied')

There are a few further indications of possible revision in addition to the line that Jonson mocked. Some are small matters that may have been sorted out at the first rehearsal, but were never adjusted in the manuscript, such as the inclusion of Lepidus in the entry direction at III.i when we would expect Ligarius, but of more significance is the question of the double reporting of Portia's death: first by Brutus himself (IV.ii.197–207), then by Messala, with Brutus denying any prior knowledge (ll. 231–45). Some critics argue that Shakespeare must have revised the scene, inserting ll. 189–212 (from the exit of the Poet to the entry of Titinius and Messala), but forgetting to delete the Messala section he had written earlier. It may be so; but other critics defend the double report in various ways as deliberate and highly dramatic. It can for instance be argued to demonstrate the stoic strength of Brutus despite his grief, or a less admirable Brutus not matching the image he has of himself. Given such disagreement, the question of revision cannot be resolved. The issue reminds us that a dramatic script is never fixed; both during the playwright's life, and even afterwards, the collaborators in the play – actors, printers, audiences, and many others – ensure that the script is always ready in potential for a new manifestation, a new enactment.

Nevertheless, the First Folio text of *Julius Caesar* is generally a very clean text, and presents few problems. It is divided into acts, but not scenes. Although it is possible that Shakespeare had a five-act structure in mind when writing, it is equally likely that the act divisions are a later addition, resulting either from the stage necessity after about 1610 of having act breaks to allow time for trimming candles in the company's new indoor theatre, or from the fashion in both theatre and printing houses for neoclassical five-act structure. When Shakespeare wrote *Julius Caesar* in 1599, his dramaturgical thinking is likely to have been most influenced by the English playhouse conception of the scene: starting and ending with a cleared stage. This is the basis for the scene division in all modern editions, and is probably the most useful starting point for thinking about the structure of the play. In the modern theatre, of course, the major element defining the structure the audience experiences is where intervals are placed, and how many there are. No interval (probably how it was originally performed), one interval, two intervals, or even more: these structure the event, and will have a powerful impact on our reaction to the play in performance.

Another crucial area for actors, audiences, and readers is punctuation. Early Modern punctuation operated by different standards to ours, and printers were much less punctilious than we would be. To take an example, here is a transcription of the First Folio version of I.i.36–43:

> O you hard hearts, you cruel men of Rome,
> Knew you not *Pompey* many a time and oft?
> Have you climb'd up to walls and battlements,
> To towers and windows? Yea, to chimney tops,
> Your infants in your arms, and there have sat
> The live-long day, with patient expectation,
> To see great *Pompey* pass the streets of Rome:
> And when you saw his chariot. . . .

Here is the same text from Arthur Humphreys's Oxford Shakespeare edition:

> O you hard hearts, you cruel men of Rome,
> Knew you not Pompey? Many a time and oft
> Have you climbed up to walls and battlements,
> To towers and windows, yea, to chimney-tops,
> Your infants in your arms, and there have sat
> The livelong day, with patient expectation,
> To see great Pompey pass the streets of Rome.
> And when you saw his chariot. . . .

It is clear enough that the Folio compositor made an error placing his first question mark after 'oft', and this may have caused the erroneous second question mark, following 'windows'. Modern editors make these corrections confidently. But the colon following 'Rome' in the second-last line of the excerpt is more difficult. Humphreys's Oxford text silently replaces the Folio colon with a full stop (as do the Oxford *Complete Works/Norton Shakespeare*, and Marvin Spevack's New Cambridge Shakespeare edition). G. Blakemore Evans's Riverside Shakespeare, however, uses a semicolon, deciding that the structure of the sentence continues, to balance what has already been said with what is about to be said. But this use of the semicolon is largely modern, and unlikely to represent either Shakespeare's writing or an Elizabethan actor's thinking. The most recent scholarly editor, David Daniell, retains Folio's colon in his Arden 3 edition (as does Norman

Sanders in his New Penguin Shakespeare), arguing that the Elizabethan use of the colon, unlike ours, can fulfil the demands of a full stop, but also serves a rhetorical need to acknowledge the forward pressure of the speech. He notes the similar use of a colon in Brutus' speech at II.i.10: 'It must be by his death: and for my part. . . .'; here Humphreys, Evans, and Sanders all substitute a semicolon, and Oxford/Norton and Spevack a full stop. But Daniell argues that 'Anything less than a colon runs the thought on too quickly: a full point destroys the appalling forward flow into speciousness' (p. 130). It is useful for actors as well as readers to be wary about how easily we accept modernized punctuation. The collaboration with the playwright should remain active.

Another crucial element for actors is the metre. While much of the dialogue is in a vigorous unadorned blank verse that offers a plain style appropriate to the austerity of Republican Rome, there is still much to be used by actors, clues to character and stage dynamics. A particularly useful tool is offered to the actor of Cassius: he is given a remarkable number of lines starting with a trochaic foot (*tum*-te) rather than the standard iambic foot (te-*tum*). The effect of this contrapuntal stress is to invite the actor to attack the line with energy, and much of the effectiveness of Cassius derives from this characteristic attacking energy:

> 'Brutus' and 'Caesar': what should be in that 'Caesar'?
> Why should that name be sounded more than yours?
> Write them together, yours is as fair a name.
> Sound them, it doth become the mouth as well.
> Weigh them, it is as heavy. Conjure with 'em,
> 'Brutus' will start a spirit as soon as 'Caesar'.
> Now in the names of all the gods at once,
> Upon what meat doth this our Caesar feed
> That his is grown so great? Age, thou art shamed!
> Rome, thou hast lost the breed of noble bloods!
>
> (I.ii.142–51)

The first line requires the initial trochee because the name Brutus is stressed on the first syllable. The second line could be spoken as an ordinary iambic pentameter, with stress on 'should'; but if the first foot is inverted, the urgency of Cassius' speech is lifted: '*Why* should that name. . . .' Then comes a string of lines starting with an attack: '*Write* them', '*Sound* them', '*Weigh* them', '*Brutus*', and probably '*Now*'. After the brief respite of the line and a half starting 'Upon what meat', Cassius uses the trochaic attack again, this time yet more forcefully. The first

half to the line, 'That his is grown so great?', is regular iambic pentameter: te-*tum*, te-*tum*, te-*tum*, almost, despite the stress on '*his*', suggesting
resignation. But it is not so. After the caesura, the pause following the
heavy punctuation in mid-line, the anticipated iamb is replaced by
a trochee before the final iamb: '*Age*, thou art *shamed!*' And the delay
between the initial trochaic stress and the following iambic stress gives
added emphasis to '*shamed*' as well. Each time Cassius uses an attacking trochee, he increases the pressure on Brutus, and impresses on the
audience how central is his energy in the play.

Such examples could be multiplied many times over. Discussion of
the text of the play serves to remind us that it is fluid, in a sense always
in process. For actors, it is the starting point towards performance, full
of clues and possibilities and potential each time the play is presented.
Spectators unfamiliar with the play experience it moment by moment,
as it unfolds, aided only by, in most cases, enough Roman history to
know that Caesar was assassinated. It was only after Shakespeare's death
that we, whether students, teachers, actors, directors, or simply literate
and interested individuals, could read and study the play as a whole
rather than experiencing it as it unfolds in time as performance.

Note

Julius Caesar is quoted and referred to in this book from the individual
Oxford Shakespeare edition edited by Arthur Humphreys, published
in 1984. In common with other *Handbooks* in this series, all references
to other Shakespeare plays are to the Oxford *Complete Works*, edited by
Stanley Wells and Gary Taylor (1986), and the *Norton Shakespeare* that is
based upon it with Stephen Greenblatt as its general editor (1997).

2   Commentary

Introduction

Although *Julius Caesar* is traditionally divided into five acts, Shakespeare did not write it in acts, but in scenes, probably pretty much as the scene divisions appear in modern editions of the play. These are 'English scenes' – scenes that continue until all characters exit, leaving the stage clear for a new scene to begin. Although some disagreement is possible over scene division, especially for the rapid shifts of the battle in Act V, generally speaking an English scene, long or short, contains a complete episode. Yet for purposes of analysis (and probably for Shakespeare when writing), it is useful to consider what we now call 'French scenes' – scenes that continue only until any character leaves the stage, or a new character enters. Act I, scene i, for instance, is a single English scene but contains at least two French scenes (three if the commoners enter prior to Flavius and Marullus). The difference in stage activity, mood, rhythm, and content between the final French scene, with just the two anxious tribunes talking alone, and the preceding confrontation with the commoners, gives a clear sense of the importance of French scenes as units of playmaking and analysis. They are also usually the basic units of rehearsal of a play.

The commentary that follows takes French scenes as the initial unit for analysis, but often needs to subdivide the French scene into what may be called 'units of action'. These units of action are usually initiated by a significant change in subject or stage dynamic. Taking I.i as an example again, when Marullus and Flavius shift at line 5 from addressing all the commoners to singling out individuals, and arguing with them, a new unit of action has started. This unit ends and a new one starts at line 32 with Marullus berating them in a long and emotional speech. And the final unit is also the new French scene of the two tribunes alone. Their exit marks the end of that unit of action, French scene, and English scene.

Awareness of French scenes and units of action will assist readers of this commentary to visualize the shift in theatrical dynamics at the point of change from one unit to another; this is the underlying structure of the play in performance.

Note: Decimal points following a line number indicate a stage direction following that line. Thus '55.2' signals the second line of a stage direction following line 55.

ACT I

Act I, scene i

1–5 Even before the confrontational energy of the first two words, 'Hence! Home', much visual information will establish the world of the play. On the Elizabethan stage the costume would be the crucial element (see pp. 4–6), but in modern productions a fictional setting is likely to show us whether we are in an austere Republican Rome, an already glorious Imperial Rome, an abstract urban setting, or a precise historical analogy such as Orson Welles's late 1930s fascist state. In an elaborate setting, there may be 'images . . . hung with Caesar's trophies' (ll. 68–9), or other indications of Caesar's power, such as the architectural inscription at Stratford in 1950 (see pp. 115–16).

Costume will do more, since it will indicate not only period, but also class and perhaps character. What kind of people are the Carpenter, Cobbler and others in their best attire, especially compared to Flavius and Marullus? Despite being tribunes of the people, Roman togas would make clear that the tribunes are members of the nobility, whereas modern productions have sometimes stressed an uneasy tension by, for instance, making them upwardly mobile trade union leaders or politicians. The commoners, however different from each other, are a group, and need to be distinct in class terms from the two tribunes. In a modern-dress production there is an opportunity here for dressing the crowd in a way likely to invite identification or association with the audience, or alternatively as a group to be observed with caution. Neither the Romans nor the Elizabethans admired mob rule.

The number of actors in the crowd will have some bearing on the scene too, as nineteenth-century productions and modern films with their huge casts demonstrate. Are there women as well as men (an innovation in the nineteenth century)? Do these commoners represent most of the population of Rome? How strong do the tribunes have to be to withstand them? And what does the acting indicate about what kind of Rome this is? Do the commoners enter with music and dancing (as at Stratford in 1950), in celebratory mode, so that the tribunes appear spoilsports? Are there already centurions or secret police in evidence as indications that dissent might be dangerous? Does the mob enter from one side of the stage to be confronted by the tribunes entering from the other? How do the commoners react to Flavius' opening speech, in blank verse, a speech both of anger at the working people for celebrating in the streets without authorization, as if this were a holiday, and of a commanding confidence in his right to demand that the commoners defer to him – note the repeated use of 'thou' to inferiors – and obey the (Elizabethan) statutes that govern costume, job, and working hours?

5–31 The Cobbler's punning jests distract and irritate the tribunes. In performance the other commoners will almost certainly be amused, and the dynamic of the scene will depend to a considerable extent on the nature of this laughter. They may be in good humour, ready to laugh easily but with no malice at the Cobbler's ability to evade the direct questions of the tribunes; they may be cautious, afraid of the tribunes; or their laughter may be drunken or malicious, perhaps foreshadowing how dangerous a mob can be if not handled carefully.

The Cobbler's role was clearly written by Shakespeare for the company clown, the stand-up comedian of the troupe. Such comedians nearly always work the audience as well as the characters of the scene they are in, so we should envisage an amiable and engaged audience by the time the Cobbler admits that he and his friends are in the streets 'to see Caesar' (ll. 30–1). At the same time, the way the Cobbler turns language inside out may not bode well for other forms of settled order.

32–60 'Wherefore rejoice?' demands Marullus, seizing the initiative back from the Cobbler, and returning the scene to blank verse with a lengthy and moving castigation of the crowd for celebrating Caesar's triumph rather than lamenting the overthrow of Pompey's 'blood' (l. 51), his sons. Civil war is no matter for rejoicing, as Plutarch makes clear (see p. 101). Marullus' speech may be angry, or may be 'more in sorrow than in anger' (*Hamlet* I.ii.229–30), which might do more to engage both audience and commoners' sympathies. Emotion is as powerful as meaning in the theatre, and initial enjoyment of the Cobbler is now balanced by more serious emotion counter to Caesar. Marullus' speech also reinforces the physical confrontation we have seen between the tribunes and the commoners. A powerful fault line runs through this Rome, with strong passions on both sides.

The reaction of the commoners is not scripted, except in Flavius' description of their exit as 'moved' and 'tongue-tied in their guiltiness' (ll. 61, 62); but other reactions are possible during the speech. If they exit the way they came (on the Elizabethan stage, by the door through which they entered), then the success of the tribunes will be strongly evident.

61 to the end   As Flavius overrides Marullus' caution about the legitimacy of stripping Caesar's images – both political danger, and sacrilege during the festival of the Lupercal – the politics become clearer. The tribunes' antagonism to Caesar is clear, and also their motive: fear that he may soar to an extraordinary height and leave them in 'servile fearfulness' (l. 75). The tribunes exit in opposite directions, further emphasizing how much they must do if they are to succeed. In some modern productions one or both have been arrested as they leave, an action that will demonstrate the power of a dictatorial Caesar, but runs the danger of making definite what Shakespeare only hints at. If the tribunes have been presented sympathetically, the audience is likely to be the more sympathetic with Cassius when news comes that they have been 'put to silence' (I.ii.282–3). The effect of this one brief scene is to bring conflict and uncertainty to the fore, and to establish a principal theme of the play: Caesar's pre-eminence, and reaction against it – and the fickle nature of the mob.

Act I, scene ii

1–11   A 'Sennet' (a flourish of trumpets) announcing Caesar's approach is very likely here as part of the ceremonial, as specified at l. 24.1. Indeed, an overlap with the preceding scene is possible: if the trumpets were heard after I.i.71, Flavius' final four lines about Caesar, and the exit of the tribunes, may have been motivated by the music of Caesar's imminent arrival. On the Elizabethan stage Caesar and the procession probably entered through the central, ceremonial door even as the tribunes exited by the two flanking doors (giving them time to tag on to the end of the procession and enter again; they are of high rank, and their silent attendance is a more subtle reminder of dissent than having them enter

under guard, as at the RSC in 1972). Even if the start of scene ii is entirely
separated from scene i by a lighting change or other means, the appearance of Caesar in such pomp is an inevitable comment on what has just
gone before.

'Peace, ho!' (l. 1) calls Casca, commanding silence from the trumpets and what may be shouting from the crowd, if they have entered as
well. Many productions add the conspirators and any other available
actors to swell the scene, and the crowd could number in the hundreds
in the nineteenth century and in films (see pp. 110–13 and p. 126). Other
extras may include soldiers and military eagles (cf. 'ensign' at V.iii.3),
lictors with their ceremonial fasces, priests, and female attendants on
Calpurnia and Portia. If so, it will be a seething and colourful crowd,
though perhaps heavily controlled, and the importance of Caesar
consequently magnified, as it is by having Casca demand quiet. The
reverse impression can be created by a limited entourage, or by Caesar appearing old or infirm (as arriving in a litter in the 1950 Stratford
production).

The important action in this sequence is Caesar commanding his
wife and Antony to use the fertility ritual of the Lupercal to try to overcome her sterility. The actor of Caesar must decide whether this is an
insight into personal and domestic distress, or a calculated political
desire to create a dynasty. Calpurnia has interesting acting options in
response, despite the lack of lines, including loving support, subser-
vient obedience, cold dislike, or embarrassment. Antony has fewer
options, but, perhaps virtually naked amongst the togas, a chance to
draw attention to himself as an ally of Caesar. Caesar, in complete control, commands the procession forward, and the trumpets no doubt
resume.

12–24 This brief sequence, in which the procession is again interrupted, and Caesar rejects the Soothsayer's warning, is so sharply
dramatized that 'Beware the Ides of March' (15 March) is one of the
best known lines in all Shakespeare. A voice 'shriller than all the
music' (l. 16) causes Caesar, characteristically referring to himself
in the third person in a distinctly Roman and particularly autocratic
manner, to command the Soothsayer before him. In some productions
the Soothsayer has been portrayed as blind, to emphasize his 'second
sight'; in some his voice is eerie and other-worldly. His second itera-
tion of 'Beware the Ides of March' (l. 23) is an incomplete line, perhaps
implying a significant pause before Caesar replies. Given Caesar's

superstition (see II.i.196) and his desire to ingratiate himself with the populace, this pause may give an impression of Caesar seriously, even politically, considering his response. In the event Caesar (unwisely, as it turns out) decides to dismiss him as a dreamer, and to resume the forward march of regular iambic pentameter, and of the procession and its shrill trumpet 'Sennet' (l. 24.1).

25–177   This extended sequence during which Cassius encourages Brutus to oppose Caesar's ever-increasing pre-eminence is in some respects an early version of Iago's famous arousal of Othello's jealousy in Othello III.iii: it is a scene of political seduction (see l. 309). Unlike Iago, however, Cassius pushes only so far, leaving Brutus to come to the final conclusion himself. The sequence unfolds in several distinct movements.

25–50   Shakespeare virtually clears the stage, thus provoking curiosity about the two men left behind: Brutus, and the somewhat older Cassius (see IV.ii.83). Brutus may be so preoccupied that Cassius actually rouses him from a reverie. Or he may stand looking thoughtfully after Caesar. Certainly Cassius takes the initiative. Brutus' explanation about holding himself aloof from the ritual is made in terms that emphasize, perhaps scornfully, how different Antony's gamesomeness is from his own reserved nature. This self-isolation is akin to Hamlet's, in a play that came soon after *Julius Caesar*. Cassius must move to intercept Brutus as he starts to leave; he then opens his campaign with a gentle complaint that his friendship is meeting a cold reception. He was Brutus' brother-in-law, but also, in Plutarch, a rival for political office. An important choice for the actor of Cassius is the extent to which he appears to be genuine in his emotion, both towards Brutus and about Caesar. He may be speaking as the thoughts come to him, surfing on his feelings; or he may have planned his tactics ahead of time, and be carefully judging his words by their effect on Brutus at each stage.

Brutus at l. 36 supplies the metrical completion of Cassius' line, perhaps interrupting what Cassius might have gone on to say. His assurance of his affection for Cassius is couched in terms of being at war with himself. Typically he has kept his worries from his friends, but we can guess that they may be concerns about the growing power of Caesar. The inwardness and self-scrutiny of Brutus is crucial to his character, and in sharp contrast to the more emotional and metrically attacking mode of Cassius (see pp. 11–12). Cassius immediately seizes on Brutus' explanation to offer thoughts that, he says, he would otherwise have hesitated to communicate. Thus Cassius has at this early stage created an emotional intimacy with Brutus that he can now use as a foundation for all that follows.

51–78   Cassius may catch the audience as well as Brutus by surprise with the indirection of his question, 'can you see your face?' (l. 51). He pursues the idea with some elaboration in a common Elizabethan formulation of the eyes and mind needing a mirror for self-understanding. Leading Romans, he says, are wishing Brutus had better vision of his own nobility. But Cassius sarcastically excepts 'immortal Caesar' (l. 60) from such well-wishing. The linking of Caesar's name with 'this age's yoke' (l. 61) is already enough for Brutus to sense danger; he may physically distance himself from Cassius, or alternatively make closer eye contact with the man who speaks what he has himself been thinking.

Cassius presses Brutus further, offering himself as Brutus' mirror. He then offers an extensive disclaimer in case Brutus should distrust him: is this a standard rhetorical ploy, or has Brutus reacted in a way that makes Cassius aware he must be cautious? Either way, Cassius emphasizes his own moderation, and contrasts the 'gentle' (l. 71; i.e. 'noble') Brutus with the falsity of 'the rout' (l. 78; 'the rabble'). This is one patrician flattering another. Cassius is interrupted, however, by the offstage sound of ceremonial trumpets and the '*shout*' (l. 78.1) of the very rabble he distrusts.

79–131   Each of the interruptions from offstage punctuates the performance; in this case Brutus may reveal his fear of what the shout means even before he utters his misgiving that they may 'Choose Caesar for their king' (l. 80). He is likely to turn towards the shout (as Booth did in 1871), and much will be revealed by the nature of the movement. Has he been on edge, half expecting it? Voting in Elizabethan parliamentary elections was by voice, so Brutus may fear election of Caesar by popular acclamation. Furthermore, Cassius' response picks up, as the audience will, that Brutus is already concerned about Caesar's ambition: 'Ay, do you fear it? / Then must I think you would not have it so' (ll. 80–1). Brutus' reply, 'I would not, Cassius, yet I love him well' (l. 82) sums up the dilemma of a patriot and a friend. A significant pause before 'yet' will underline not only the difficulty Brutus faces, but also the engagement of emotion as well as reason. The line may be as much an introspective admission to himself as a response to Cassius.

That Brutus may have revealed more than he intended is suggested by his sudden return to more formal language in the next line. This shift might be emphasized by movement to a different position on stage. At the same time, his immediate comment on the importance of honour, even if it should lead to death, may suggest a continuing preoccupation with the dilemma of Caesar's possible aspiration to tyrannical control. For Brutus 'honour' is for 'the general good' (l. 85). For Cassius, in contrast, honour, which he claims is 'the subject of my story' (l. 92), seems more to do with personal reputation and standing, and is perhaps motivated by envy of 'such a thing as myself' (l. 96) holding a higher position. Cassius does not wish to 'bend his body' (l. 117), to bow to another man. How bitter Cassius is about Caesar will have a significant bearing in performance on how he tells Brutus the two anecdotes that now follow.

In the first, starting 'For once, upon a raw and gusty day' (l. 100), Cassius depicts himself as a bold and friendly competitor with Caesar, accepting a dare to swim the Tiber in flood. Not only does he win the dare, but even has to rescue Caesar from drowning. Cassius scornfully mimics Caesar's pathetic plea for help, and compares his own strength and success with that of the mythical founder of Rome, Aeneas. The point, of course, is to emphasize that Caesar is no more than a mortal as they are, and a weak one at that. Readers of Plutarch who heard this in the theatre would know that Cassius was painting a different picture from the historical version, and that would underline what appears to be personal envy lying behind the attack (cf. V.v.71).

Whether the second story, starting 'He had a fever' (l. 119), now suddenly occurs to Cassius as a result of his getting caught up in his own emotion, or is a more calculated reaction to Brutus' silent attitude, will be important for our feelings about Cassius (see reference to Gielgud's performance in 1950, p. 114). The anecdote of Caesar's fever again accentuates Caesar's supposed weakness (with, again, the scornful mimicry), and, like the first, ends with reference to the unreasonableness of such a weak individual becoming 'a god' (l. 116) who may 'bear the palm alone' (l. 131).

132–61 A second interruption by trumpets and shouting arouses Brutus' anxiety about what powers Caesar may be given, and, since the diversion breaks the conversation, gives Cassius an opportunity to continue in a more personal and intimate way, as if something had now been agreed between them, with brilliant and instinctive oratory.

'The fault, dear Brutus, is not in our stars' (l. 140), says Cassius, rejecting
a belief in fate (cf. IV.ii.268–74), and instead insisting that the responsibility to act against the 'colossus' (l. 136) is theirs. The skill of Cassius' verse in this passage has been discussed above (see pp. 11–12), but
we should note also the rhetorical dexterity of the way he juxtaposes the
names of Caesar and Brutus. He probably uses a large physical gesture to
imply the weighing of them, almost juggling the two names in his hands.

Directors and editors have puzzled over the discrepancy between
only two shouts being specified in stage directions despite Cassius
and Casca both saying the mob 'shouted thrice' (ll. 225–41). In Plutarch the crown was only offered twice (see p. 102), and Shakespeare
may have wanted only two shouts so as to divide this long sequence
into equal thirds between the exit and return of Caesar. Consistency
is an obsession of modern realists, who sometimes misunderstand
Shakespearean dramaturgy. However, it is possible that a stage direction for a third shout is missing, perhaps following l. 147, in which
case the renewed shouting motivates Cassius' increased anger starting at l. 148. He invokes 'Rome' five times in ten lines (six if we count
the 'Rome/room' pun at l. 156), and finishes with Brutus' celebrated
Republican ancestor, Junius Brutus, who, says Cassius, would no more
have allowed the devil to rule Rome than a king. The implication for
what his friend Brutus should do is clear.

162–77 Brutus' manner contrasts sharply with that of Cassius.
Whereas Cassius' speech is always pressing forward, the incomplete
last line implies a pause for reflection before Brutus speaks. When he
does, his rhetoric is controlled, calm, and balanced (ll. 162–5). Brutus
may use 'For this present' (l. 165) to pre-empt an intended interruption
by Cassius. He demands time to think, but is likely in his body language
and gesture to reveal evidence of mental and emotional turmoil that his
natural instinct is to suppress. He wishes to display what the Romans
called 'gravitas'. His final statement before the return of Caesar is hardly
revolutionary, but Cassius is probably accurate in thinking it a 'show /
Of fire' (ll. 176–7), if a minor one, from so controlled a man as Brutus.
This long sequence between the two men, which started at l. 25, gives us
no clear indication of what Brutus will eventually decide, but Cassius'
intention has become clear, and his speech has suffered no rebuff.

178–89 The return of Caesar and his train is a major change in the
stage dynamic. While it is possible that the entry direction is slightly

early, and that Brutus is first alerted to Caesar's return by a trumpet 'sennet' (see l. 24.1 and 214.1), the absence of a fanfare is in keeping with Caesar's anger and the anxiety of everyone else. Possibly Marullus and Flavius are no longer present, having been 'put to silence' (ll. 282–3). The stage arrangement is significant: clearly Brutus and Cassius are at a distance from all the others, allowing them to comment, by stage convention, unheard, on Caesar. But the physical space also carries meaning in itself, especially after what has gone before. This sense of separation is emphasized by Cassius suggesting what sounds like a surreptitious manner of ensuring Casca stays behind (for the 'sleeve', l. 179, see p. 5).

190–214 As Caesar summons Antony they may both move away slightly from the rest, or Caesar's followers may discreetly fall back; more important, however, is that the separation between Cassius and Brutus on the one hand and everyone else on the other continues, and may appear almost emblematic. Since Caesar speaks about Cassius alone, it is possible that Brutus has briefly moved to join someone in the main group, perhaps Portia. Whatever their exact position, Caesar has dominated the stage picture since his entry, and his tone here is important to our reaction. If he is entirely serious about his fear of anyone with 'a lean and hungry look' like Cassius (l. 194), there is a danger he will sound foolish and pompous. He is more likely perhaps to be partly joking, partly serious, and it may be (deliberately) difficult for us to determine the balance. Certainly the rest of his commentary on Cassius sounds intelligent, and matches what we have already seen and heard; compare, for instance, ll. 208–9 with ll. 94–9, 115–18. Antony underestimates Cassius just as Brutus earlier underestimated Antony, but Caesar recognizes the danger. Presumably Caesar's complaint about Cassius smiling seldom, and as if in mockery when he does, will be an accurate reflection of the acting of Cassius, just as the casting should not provide a fat actor for the role.

Caesar's accurate estimation of Cassius is weakened by the arrogance of his insistence that his name is not 'liable to fear', perhaps nettled by Antony's implication that Caesar does fear him (cf. II.ii.32–7, 44–8), and the insistence that 'always I am Caesar' (l. 212). Further, we are reminded of Cassius' report of his physical inadequacy by the colossus Caesar admitting to deafness. As they set off again, with trumpets this time, we will see Brutus quietly hold Casca back.

215–91 Casca, dressed in the same clothing of the Roman nobility as Cassius and Brutus, affects a different manner from them. Cassius has already warned Brutus of Casca's 'sour fashion' (l. 180), and this is revealed in various ways. He speaks prose throughout. His humour is always rough and offhand (such as his impolite reaction to Cassius' dinner invitation), sometimes brutal (as in his casual joke that he should have killed Caesar when he offered his throat to be cut). Despite his plebeian language, his scorn for the 'rabblement' (l. 242) is palpable, strongly expressed through a physical disgust at their chapped hands, the smell of their breath and sweat, and the noise of their shouting, clapping, and hissing. The actor has an important decision to make about the extent to which he makes the character appear a coherent personality, or alternatively allows it to be seen that Casca is adopting a blunt, malcontent, sarcastic, jokey persona that hides whatever he really thinks. Perhaps he feels a need to impress Brutus, who is all that he is not.

The audience as much as Brutus and Cassius will be eager for Casca's report on what has happened offstage. That Caesar should have been offered a crown instantly recalls Brutus' fear that the people may be choosing Caesar as a king. It is Brutus who initiates the rapid-fire questioning of Casca; Brutus and Cassius may be simply urgent in their questions, or they may exchange a glance that will confirm their shared sense of the seriousness of this development. Casca's brief hint about each putting by of the crown being 'gentler than other' (l. 229), and the information that Antony offered the crown (suggesting that Caesar has stage-managed the whole event) lead to Brutus' possibly frustrated demand for more detail: 'Tell us the manner of it, gentle Casca' (l. 233). Casca claims that it was 'mere foolery; I did not mark it' (l. 235), and in some productions has only offered more detail when restrained from leaving by Brutus and Cassius, and then only to placate them with something he declares to have been unimportant. This may be an act by Casca. At any rate, he sketches crucial points with great immediacy: Caesar reluctantly refusing the crown three times, the mob cheering him enthusiastically each time he refused, and Caesar fainting in what Brutus identifies as an epileptic fit ('the falling sickness', l. 252).

Cassius seizes the phrase in a metaphorical sense to claim that the three of them have, politically, 'the falling sickness' (l. 254), not Caesar, who is by implication rising. Again, Cassius may exchange a significant glance with Brutus, or there may be a pause to see if either Brutus or Casca will respond. If so, the silence will be laden with political potential. Casca, however, feigns stupidity and carelessness. Does he give any sense of being intimidated by Brutus? Or is he unwilling to speak until he has conferred with Cassius privately? Whatever his reasons, he acts as if he doesn't care, while at the same time describing the plebeians as clapping or hissing Caesar just as if he were an actor in the theatre. Spoken by an actor in a theatre, these lines constitute an audacious risk for Shakespeare. He is deliberately reminding his audience that they are in a playhouse, that what they are watching is a version of a historical event that is also, here, a fiction. This self-referentiality is akin to what Bertolt Brecht was to do in the twentieth century: encouraging an audience to think about what they were watching, as well as enjoying it. Often now called metatheatre, this technique allows the theatre to use itself as a metaphor.

What follows is Casca's sardonic description of Caesar's play-acting to the crowd, Caesar's lack of pleasure about the whole episode, a joke about Cicero speaking in Greek to his well-educated friends (a discreet political caution), and that the tribunes Marullus and Flavius have been 'put to silence' (in Plutarch, loss of office, not death: see p. 102). Again, the reaction of Brutus and Cassius to this new evidence of the dangers of resisting Caesar will be significant. It may be silence, or an exchange of glances, or Brutus may react differently from Cassius. Casca may or may not give evidence of understanding the implication of what he has just said. He simply starts to say farewell, and gives the impression of not thinking a meal with Cassius urgent, though Cassius' invitation may imply previous private meetings between the two. As he leaves the stage, the fallout from what he has just said hangs heavy in the air.

292–304   Cassius assures Brutus that Casca's apparent slow-wittedness is simply a façade, and that he is quick and sharp and practical in any 'bold or noble' (l. 295) undertaking. This choice of words will appeal to Brutus. Whereas he earlier put Cassius off (l. 165–70), now he initiates a meeting for tomorrow. This increased urgency implies a greater commitment to what Cassius has hinted at. And Cassius, to cap 'bold or noble', adds, perhaps interrupting Brutus' exit to give more weight to the line, 'think of the world' (l. 304). Again, an appeal to duty is designed precisely for the serious-minded and public-spirited Brutus.

305 to the end   For the first time in the play a single character is alone on stage, reflecting on all the action of a long scene. The first few lines are addressed as if to Brutus, using the intimate (or slightly con-descending) singular forms 'thou' and 'thy' (ll. 305–6). In an elaborate set of alchemical puns on 'noble' and 'mettle' (ll. 305–6), Cassius speaks of working Brutus' high-minded temperament as if it were soft metal like gold, but, counter to alchemical aims, for the purpose of distorting it from its usual honourable disposition. Although critics suggest that the seduction of Brutus to which Cassius refers at l. 309 can work two ways, referring both to the danger of Brutus being seduced by Caesar's blandishments as well as succumbing to the persuasions of Cassius, an actor cannot play two opposite objectives at the same time. It seems much the more likely that Cassius is continuing his observation that he has just proven Brutus can be moulded.

At this point Cassius becomes more emphatic in his delivery, start-ing with 'Caesar doth bear me hard' at l. 310. This probably marks the beginning of direct address to the audience in place of the earlier think-ing aloud as he seemed to address Brutus. If so, the audience now in a sense becomes complicit with Cassius as he shares his pleasure at per-suading Brutus towards active opposition to Caesar. And Cassius con-fides his intention to undertake various political dirty tricks to further influence Brutus. A rhyming couplet gives a sense of completion to the scene as Cassius exits with great confidence in their ability, if Brutus joins them, to unseat Caesar.

Act I, scene iii

1–2 The thunder and lightning follows immediately upon Cassius' exit lines about shaking Caesar, and might be quite spectacular. The charac-ters may be wearing cloaks or other outdoor clothing. However, Cicero, the famous and learned senate orator mentioned in the previous scene, seems unperturbed. We learn from his question that it is evening, and this might also be evident from Cicero, for instance, carrying a lantern, or from dim lighting in modern productions. Furthermore, Casca is carrying a drawn sword; since Cicero makes no comment on it, the actors need to decide whether Casca carries it unobtrusively until l. 19, or if Cicero's Roman calm extends to ignoring drawn weapons (which would make him appear the more remarkable). Almost certainly the two men meet after entering from opposite sides of the stage (see pp. 3–4), and Cicero could play the darkness to make clear why it is only at l. 2 that he notices Casca's breathlessness and staring eyes. Casca may have entered running, perhaps looking over his shoulder in fright, before encountering (bumping into?) the calm Cicero.

3–40   This is a new Casca, quite unlike the mordant and self-confident jester of I.ii. He paints a vivid word picture of a world being shaken to its foundations, and employs words like 'ambitious', 'swell', 'exalted', and 'threatening' (ll. 7–8) that could imply Caesar. The question for the actor is whether Casca intends to use the storm as a political allegory for Caesarism in order to sound out Cicero, or whether Casca's real fear of the storm and the portents he describes provide Shakespeare an opportunity to make Casca an unwitting conveyor of language that the audience may by now be attuned to associating with Caesar. Casca's physical agitation will probably add to an audience's sense of instability. Casca regards the storm as evidence of disturbance among the gods that may presage destruction on earth, and he seems deeply impressed by the prodigies he has seen or heard about. He believes they are portents, heralding dire results (see p. 102). The association of domestic and political disorder with cosmic disorder had a long tradition, going back to medieval theatre; and Shakespeare, drawing on the Latin poet Ovid, had dramatized it in his own earlier plays, and was to do so most memorably in *King Lear*.

Cicero appears to counter all this with a straightforward dismissal of superstition, but his comment about it being 'a strange-disposèd time' (l. 33) might be a political comment as well (spoken with caution; compare his use of Greek reported in I.ii). His interest in Caesar's intention to attend the Capitol the next day adds to our sense of an increasing pace to events.

41–115   *In the course of this sequence an excited Cassius draws Casca to believe that he will kill himself rather than live under the tyranny of Caesar, thus putting Casca in a situation where he has to declare himself.*

41–5   Cassius' 'Who's there' emphasizes the darkness of the scene, the anxiety of both men, and perhaps the reversal (as in these same words opening *Hamlet*) of the normal pattern of the newcomer waiting to be challenged. The quick, nervous interchange of l. 41 leads to mutual recognition, and Casca reiterating the same fear about the storm that he revealed to Cicero, only to be cut short by a confident Cassius who instantly and explicitly links the storm to the political situation 'so full of faults' (l. 45).

46–71 Cassius seems to have been exhilarated by the storm (and perhaps by his plotting gathering momentum, and maybe by now initiating an attempt to have Casca commit himself), and his 'unbracèd' (l. 48; – 'unfastened') clothing will give him a wild appearance (cf. Hamlet, 'with his doublet all unbraced', II.i.79). Although a rationalist to the extent of criticizing Casca's irrational fear of the storm (ll. 57–61), Cassius' defiance of the heavens, baring his chest to the lightning bolt, suggests a titanic struggle between man and Roman gods or Christian God. He goes on to describe the portents in terms even more extreme than those of Casca: he says that the natural order has changed from its ordained character, and now has become 'monstrous' (l. 68); that is, deformed and unnatural. When he says this must all foretell a 'monstrous state' (l. 71), he both reinforces Casca's unfocused fear of a horrendous condition to come, and also implies that the 'state' of Rome may have become deformed. Thus Cassius has in one sense overridden Casca's intellectual uncertainty about the storm and portents, but in an emotional sense has reinforced and even expanded Casca's alarm at the state of affairs in heaven and earth; on both counts he has, therefore, established an ascendency over Casca.

72–84 Cassius now tests Casca more closely by offering to 'name to thee a man' (l. 72) who is as 'dreadful' and 'prodigious' (ll. 73, 77) as the storm and its portents. Perhaps Cassius emphasizes the need for his indirect speech by drawing Casca away from any conceivable eavesdroppers. He is clearly dangling the bait in front of Casca. Casca, with characteristic bluntness, answers this elaborate secrecy with a direct conclusion that Cassius means Caesar, followed by the request for confirmation, 'Is it not, Cassius?' (l. 79). Given Cassius' retreat into mystery in the next line ('Let it be who it is'), perhaps there is a pause in the middle of l. 79 that prompts Casca's demand that Cassius confirm what is of course apparent to them both. It seems that Cassius wants Casca to come to him, rather than the reverse; hence his continuation of general bewailing of the supine willingness of Romans to submit to oppression.

85–111 Casca knows they are talking about Caesar, and reveals that the planned crowning of Caesar as king outside Italy is to take place in the Senate tomorrow. Cassius again responds with intense rhetoric and emotion about suicide (admirable in a Roman, sinful for an Elizabethan Christian) as a release from tyranny. He probably draws 'this dagger' to illustrate his intention, just as Casca may still have his sword in his hand from earlier in the scene. (If he has already sheathed it, Casca will at least gesture to it again at l. 101.) Just as Cassius speaks of shaking off tyranny, the stage direction *'Thunder still'* (l. 100) is a reminder that inter-mittent sounds of the fearful storm are still heard still heard, perhaps punctuating the structure of the dialogue.

Cassius ratchets up the emotional intensity, but also the politi-cal implications about whose duty it is to act, with a lament for the state of Roman citizens, whose servility is to blame for Caesar's pre-eminence. Again, the actor of Cassius must choose how much this kind of speech is a genuine outpouring of the man's emotional despair for Rome or hatred of Caesar, or how much a carefully calculated ensnar-ing of Casca. It probably has elements of both; the question is, in what proportions?

111–15 Cassius' sudden apparent realization that he has said too much, that his words constitute treason for which Casca could denounce him, sound very much like a carefully constructed charade that will require Casca to declare himself one way or the other. Cassius will have to try to imbue this apparent lapse with enough emotional intensity to make it look plausible to Casca. He may even raise the dagger to give the 'answer' he will make if Casca is hostile – suicide – an immediate threat in stage terms.

116–30 Casca evidently recognizes Cassius' play-acting for the dan-gerous invitation it is, for he instantly declares he is ready to commit himself up to the hilt to whatever faction has been formed. He sounds relieved to have things out in the open; ll. 116–17 may even contain a hint of reprimand that Cassius has gone through such verbal contor-tions to test him. Certainly Casca offers his hand (perhaps needing first to sheathe his sword), and if he matches the verbal parallel of 'hand' and 'foot' (ll. 117, 119) with physical extension of both, his posture will be heroic.

Cassius no doubt takes his hand to seal the 'bargain' (l. 120), and certainly abandons his rhetoric as he quickly outlines the cur-rent state of the conspiracy: several other high-minded Romans, an object both honourable and dangerous, and a meeting established for this very night at 'Pompey's Porch' (l. 126). Pompey was of course Caesar's enemy, so the portico of his 'Theatre' (152; see p. 92) seems as appropriate to the meeting as the 'bloody-fiery' night (l. 130). In the space of a few moments on stage, a conspiracy has been revealed, its plans imminent.

131–52 The arrival of Cinna 'in haste' (l. 131; just as both Casca and Cassius may have been as they entered) adds to the sense of time speeding up that is characteristic of this entire scene. It is still dark, and Casca both emphasizes this (usefully, on the Elizabethan stage) and his practicality as a conspirator by drawing Cassius into concealment ('Stand close', l. 131) and readiness for danger until Cassius can recognize and greet Cinna. The newcomer cannot identify the figure with Cassius in the 'dark', thinking it must be 'Metellus Cimber' (l. 134). This, combined with Cassius' question about Decius Brutus and Trebonius (l. 148), identifies for Casca (and the audience) further members of the conspiracy – as it turns out, the full membership apart from Brutus.

Cinna displays nervousness in his failure to answer Cassius' question at l. 136, and his Casca-like concern about the storm and portents. Cassius brings Cinna up short by repeating the question about whether the others are waiting for him, and then interrupts him when he launches into a passionate hope that Brutus can be won over to the conspiracy. Is Cinna frightened, perhaps anxious about Cassius as a leader, or simply ineffectual? Cassius calms him down by giving him practical tasks: he is to deliver several anonymous messages where Brutus will find them. In Plutarch these messages were the spontaneous work of various hands; here, Cassius is masterminding the entire conspiracy, and especially the enlisting of 'the noble Brutus'.

153 to the end In the final sequence of the scene, in which Cassius initiates the move towards Brutus' house, Casca seconds Cinna's sense of the importance of Brutus to their cause. Just as in Plutarch (see p. 90), Brutus is universally recognized as a man of utter integrity; Cassius agrees with Casca that this nobility of mind and reputation is vital if their cause is to appear just. As Cassius reveals that the night is more than half over already, we again have a sense of events unfolding at an increasing tempo. The scene started with almost philosophical reflections on a storm; now a conspiracy has been revealed, and three of its members are in urgent action towards securing Brutus by the end of the night.

ACT II

Act II, scene i

1–9   Brutus, just eulogized by the exiting Casca and Cassius, is probably dressed and therefore in a sense ready for the new day (in contrast to Caesar in the next scene), but he is, as Cassius was, 'unbracèd' (l. 263). It is still night, since Brutus in his garden can see the stars, but presumably there is no more thunder. As he calls offstage for Lucius, he reveals to the audience, either wearily, or often as a gentle joke about the young, that he has himself been sleepless.

The boy Lucius may well be quite sleepy, and the concern Brutus shows for him throughout the scene tends to show a gentle human side of Brutus, a useful glimpse beyond his always rational exterior. Nevertheless, it is evident that Brutus is up and about with purpose, and intending to work in his study.

10–34   The suddenness of 'It must be by his death' (l. 10) will shock the audience. When Brutus was last seen, he promised to think about the threat of Caesar; clearly he can have done little else since, and we now understand that his sleepless night has been occupied with this thought. What is even more surprising is that Brutus seems to have reached a conclusion already. For the actor, the rest of the soliloquy, which justifies this conclusion, probably needs to be charged with an emotional reluctance to admit the logic of the case; or, alternatively, an emotional need to persuade himself that his conclusion really is noble. Over it all hangs a recollection of how Cassius 'did whet me against Caesar' (l. 61). Brutus, in deep thought, may well on the Elizabethan stage have 'walked about, / Musing, and sighing, with [his] arms across', as Portia describes his disturbed behaviour at II.i.238–9.

Brutus proceeds in the grave manner we expect of him, first laying out the 'question' (l. 13), as Hamlet was famously to do in Shakespeare's next tragedy, the precise matter requiring deliberation. Brutus' opposition, he says, has no personal basis, but only concern for the general good. As he considers the matter, he does not limit himself, as Cassius did in his soliloquy, to ways and means, but weighs the moral issues. Here Brutus must persuade the audience of his integrity, even if we are allowed to see the dangers of unacknowledged rationalization behind his reasoning. The argument develops on the basis that the power of kingship would probably corrupt any man and lead to tyranny. Thus, although Brutus acknowledges that he has never known Caesar to allow his passions to overrule his good judgement, it is entirely possible he would as king, and therefore he must be stopped.

Despite this conclusion, Brutus fairly acknowledges that Caesar's current behaviour will not appear to justify assassination, and that he will need to 'Fashion' (l. 30) the justification. Rather than simply saying 'So Caesar *may*', he will need to say that he '*would* as his kind grow mischievous' (ll. 27, 33; my italics). Thus, despite his logical conclusion that Caesar must be killed for the general good, Brutus unwittingly reveals the weakness of an argument that will 'bear no colour' (l. 29) as the thing it is, but will instead need careful manipulation: what we now call political 'spin'.

35–43 When Lucius returns with a mysterious letter (which the audience knows must be one of those delivered by Cinna), Brutus intends to send him to bed, since it is not yet day. But Brutus recalls that the day will be significant. In Folio he asks if tomorrow is 'the first of March'. Probably 'first' is a printing error for 'Ides' (l. 40; the fifteenth of the month), which Lucius confirms at l. 59, although Plutarch mentions both dates (see pp. 90, 92). Either way, Brutus' awareness of the pressure of time leads to checking the calendar, and to an emphasis for the audience on the repetition of the Soothsayer's warning in I.ii.

44–58 Alone again, Brutus uses the unearthly light to read the letter. He is by now familiar with these anonymous instigations, and the audience will recognize Cassius' return to the image of Brutus needing to see himself; in addition, Brutus' piecing out of the hints in the letter follows precisely the formulation of Cassius at I.ii.151–61, including the appeal to Brutus' heroic Republican ancestor who drove out the last kings of Rome, the Tarquins. By now Brutus has satisfied himself through abstract reasoning of the legitimacy of action, and therefore commits himself. Since the declaration is in a soliloquy, the audience will accept its absolute sincerity.

59–60 As if cued by Brutus' promise, Lucius returns to confirm that the day to come is indeed the Ides of March; and a knock is heard. Brutus may show surprise at such early callers; more likely, and dramatically richer for the actor, is a fatalistic realization of who it must be. His decision is already attended with its consequence. The reaction of Lucius, constantly in and out in this scene, to Brutus may assist audience understanding of the moment.

61–9 Brutus' soliloquy will be brief, since visitors are at the door; this further intensifies the speech. In addition, Brutus' statement that he has not slept since Cassius sharpened him like an instrument against Caesar implies, like his familiarity with anonymous letters (ll. 50–1), a double time scheme: a slow accumulation of reflection and pressure over an extended period, and the intense pressure of events since we saw Cassius first broach the question and send such letters less than twenty-four hours earlier. Realistically, one or other must be wrong. But the actor can avoid the trap of realism by adopting both aspects as emotionally true, thus enriching the dramaturgical density of the moment.

Brutus reveals a tragic torment of mind very similar to that Shakespeare later gives Macbeth (I.iii.136–41), in which the period between the decision to act and the act itself has the unreality of a nightmare. The soul and body seem to be in a fierce debate; in an analogy familiar to Elizabethans, the human state resembles both the political (a 'little kingdom' in civil 'insurrection'; ll. 68–9) and the cosmic. Brutus is here at his most vulnerable, revealing the depths of feeling and sensitivity that at other times are cloaked by his gravity and reason.

70–85 Brutus' premonition about the identity of his visitors is confirmed as he twice asks Lucius for further information, not believing that it will be only his brother-in-law Cassius. Lucius' hesitation may be prompted by understandable suspicion of this band of men who have so muffled their faces with hats and cloaks as to be unrecognizable. Brutus understands immediately who they are, and his first response is to acknowledge the shame of involvement in conspiracy: the 'monstrous' (l. 81) nature of such treachery. What makes it worse is the need for hypocrisy, for false smiles. As Hamlet was to say, 'one may smile and smile and be a villain' (I.v.109), and Brutus feels the stain of the path he has chosen.

86–100 The five men following Cassius are probably muffled as previously described; although there is no stage direction for Lucius to appear, in production he may be seen, and his attitude be evident before he retires. Other decisions are needed too: whether Brutus is at a distance, perhaps still preoccupied with the thoughts of ll. 77–85; how public or personal Cassius' greeting is; whether Brutus asks 'Know I these men' (l. 89) as an aside to Cassius (as Booth did in 1871), or if instead he speaks aloud as a friendly host, adopting 'smiles and affability' (l. 82) to show them all by example how they must behave. Cassius' reply as he starts to introduce them seems likely to be aloud, not only repeating his insistence to Brutus of how much he is looked to by other Romans, but also setting the tone and agenda for the other conspirators. Do they all unmuffle themselves at this point, or one by one as they are introduced? Are they confident or embarrassed? Does Brutus greet them in a friendly and personal way, perhaps shaking hands, or is he distant and cool? The relaxed formality with which he asks them why they have come (ll. 98–9) could fit with either. Cassius then draws Brutus aside for a word in private, leaving the conspirators the rest of the stage.

101–11 This brief interlude draws attention to time passing and dawn's imminence, reminds the audience of what is to occur at the Capitol in the morning, and provides the symbolism of Casca pointing his drawn sword at where Caesar will appear. The tone of the discussion will determine whether or not a lack of harmony among the conspirators is also intended. Although productions have occasionally abandoned the geographical debate in favour of Casca indicating Brutus as their rising sun, this may seem somewhat melodramatic, and it certainly fails to divert audience attention from Cassius and Brutus as is required (unless, as in the Mankiewicz film (see pp. 126–8), Casca's speech finishes as he points his sword at Brutus on 'Here . . . the sun arises' (l. 106).

112–92 *As Brutus assumes leadership of the conspiracy, he overrides Cassius on three important issues: a proposed oath, enlisting Cicero, and dealing with Mark Antony. The reaction of Cassius and the other conspirators to Brutus' high moral tone is of great significance.*

112–13 Brutus returns to the group as a confirmed member of the conspiracy. Shakespeare has no need of realistic time for Brutus to explain this to Cassius in the previous ten lines, since the audience knows the details of Brutus' journey to this point. What matters is that Brutus is committed, and his action of shaking hands with each man again will take stage time that seals the agreement.

114–40 Brutus' first act as a conspirator is to contradict Cassius and assume leadership through moral virtue. The reasons he gives for not swearing an oath are simple. First, the conspirators have motive enough already: the way men look up to them, the deep distress they themselves are feeling, and the objective evidence of the evils of the time (ll. 114–15). In addition, Brutus asks why they need an oath, since they are honourable Romans, not priests, cowards, crafty cautious men, or spineless victims. Brutus implies again that being Roman raises them to a special level of honour, virtue, and loyalty. See p. 91.

The speech is heightened by passionate rhetoric. Apart from the short, decisive start, 'No, not an oath' (l. 114), his sentences are all long, clause sweeping after uninterrupted clause as he exhorts the conspirators towards the essential nobility of their act. The vocabulary does the same job: fire, steel, spur, valour, honesty, and virtue to describe themselves: idle, cowards, feeble carrions, guilty, and bastardy for those who would not comport themselves as true Romans. The passion is strengthened by his double use of the emphatic form, 'this shall be, or we will fall for it' (l. 128), rather than the plain statement: 'this will be, or we shall fall for it.' Elizabethan English still deployed these alternatives with force in a way that modern English has almost lost.

In the event the conspiracy is not betrayed by refusing an oath. However, the audience does not know yet that it will not be, and the danger is amply foregrounded here. Perhaps more important, Brutus displays not the slightest sense that he should discuss the matter with Cassius or the others. His ethical standards are principled and absolute, and he seems to take it for granted that the others will acknowledge that he is right. It will be a significant production decision how the more pragmatic Cassius and the others will respond – during, and especially at the end – to the speech. In particular, what is the quality of the pause (if there is one) before Cassius speaks?

141–54 Cassius does not respond to the high rhetoric of Brutus; instead, in a short speech (whose abruptness may itself carry a comment) he proposes they find out if Cicero will join them. Casca and Metellus second this enthusiastically, the latter pointing out the benefits of acquiring such a respected and senior figure because they will need the people's 'good opinion' (l. 154). Brutus, however, for the second time rejects Cassius' advice. Cassius accedes, but Casca agrees with an emphasis that draws attention to his reversal. Is Casca overdoing loyalty to Cassius? Is he awed by Brutus? Is he naturally variable, a lightweight? Folio's three short lines (ll. 152–4; Brutus' final half line, and both Cassius' and Casca's) imply either three pauses, or a full line and a half line, which would either leave a pause after Brutus' speech, with Casca quickly completing Cassius' line, or Cassius smoothly following Brutus, in which case an uncomfortable pause may follow Casca's conspicuous turnaround.

155–92 After the possible awkward silence following Casca's line, Decius introduces a third and vital question in a more diplomatic manner. Cassius seizes on it (have they previously discussed this?), and urges the death of Mark Antony for the pragmatic reason that he is likely to be their main threat if they leave him alive. For the third time Brutus opposes Cassius. Again adopting a tone of high ethical principle, he urges all the conspirators to ensure that they act, and be seen to act, only from the highest principles of justice. They should be, in effect, priests carrying out a necessary sacrifice for the health of the body politic (note 'purgers', l. 181, a medical term). 'Let us be sacrificers, but not butchers' (l. 167), says Brutus, 'carve him as a dish fit for the gods' (l. 174). Furthermore, he says, Antony will be powerless once Caesar is dead.

Brutus' need to exalt the act, and his distaste for the bloody reality of murder, is clear from the revealing and slightly cynical suggestion that they allow their hearts to instigate the killing, then chide themselves afterwards, just as masters may rebuke their followers afterwards for carrying out violent acts they incited. Depending on the acting of Brutus, and the response of the other conspirators, the audience may be partly aware of this dark underside of conspiracy, while at the same time being swept up in the nobility of Brutus' convictions; or may be encouraged to sense some grotesquerie in the concept of carving Caesar at a heavenly banquet. To undermine the high ideals of Brutus too much, however, carries severe risks for later in the play.

This time Cassius refuses to back down, and starts to urge the danger of Antony. When Brutus interrupts and overrides him, the reaction of Cassius will be important. Does he display irritation? Or, perhaps more telling, does he acquiesce, but still give evidence of being troubled and unpersuaded? In the event, he will be proven tragically correct about Antony, and establishing his feelings strongly with the audience now will have a payoff later. Brutus may realize that he is not persuading Cassius, and his final two lines (ll. 189–90) may seek from all the conspirators an easy laugh in denigrating Antony as a mere playboy, not to be taken seriously. That Trebonius rather than Cassius replies tends to support such a staging, which will in effect block Cassius from continuing to argue.

192.1　The stage direction '*Clock strikes*' reminds us of Shakespeare's concern with the pressure of time in this part of the play. The scene started when it was 'not day' (l. 39), the conspirators discussed whether or not they could discern dawn on the horizon (ll. 101–11), and now dawn and the start of the Elizabethan working day approach. If the clock strikes the quarters prior to the three slow notes of the hour, the stage picture will in effect freeze to a tableau as they wait.

193–229　Since people will soon be up and about, the conspirators must disperse. But Cassius raises a concern about whether or not Caesar will attend that day's Senate meeting at (in the play, if not historically) the Capitol, citing Caesar's growing superstition which may keep him at home. Again, Cassius is constantly aware of the practicalities of assassination. What is also now assumed, though it has never been stated, is that the attempt will be made that very day.

Decius' description of Caesar as loving to hear of unnatural natural history, and his vanity in being flattered by being told he hates flatterers, paints an unflattering portrait of a man with flaws of judgement more serious than the physical weakness that so incensed Cassius in I.ii. The speech may also confirm an audience sense of Decius as a smooth and persuasive operator: useful to the conspiracy, but hardly adding to its nobility.

They all agree to meet Decius at Caesar's house by eight, but before they leave Metellus suggests that Caius Ligarius might be an ally, since he bears a grudge against Caesar, and for once Brutus agrees. As Cassius urges them all to be true, Brutus adds his own conviction (see ll. 77–85) that they must put on a mask of cheerfulness in public lest they betray themselves. Indeed, they must stay in character ('formal constancy', l. 228) 'as our Roman actors do' (l. 227), another overt reminder to the audience that what they are viewing is a theatrical reconstruction of history, but also a view of history in which the leading figures had parts to play. Finally, Brutus wishes them all 'good morrow' (l. 229), another reminder that the night is over and a significant day is dawning.

230–4　Although Lucius is not identified in Folio as being on stage, many productions have had him asleep somewhere in the background to add to the sentiment of Brutus now leaving him to sleep. Unlike Lucius, Brutus admits to being beset with illusions and phantasms rather than enjoying healthful sleep. The audience may relate this admission to the meeting that has just finished, which has not only kept Brutus awake, but is also in itself preparation for an unnatural act of killing.

234–7   Portia's entry is a striking contrast to the conspirators who have just left. She will be in night-clothes, a reminder of the abnormality of the night-time meeting of the fully dressed conspirators we have just seen. Brutus' reaction is agitated, initially seeming to blame her for her presence (no doubt because his mind is on secrecy), then with real concern, or perhaps covering up his first response, urging her to avoid the 'vile contagion' (l. 266) of the night in her 'weak condition' (l. 237). In performance, the actress may accept this as an Elizabethan cultural assumption about women's supposed weakness, both physical and mental (see Cassius' pejorative use of 'womanish' at I.iii.84), which then adds power to her own 'I grant I am a woman, but . . .' at ll. 293, 295). Alternatively, she may follow Plutarch in exhibiting physical frailty (see p. 93), or as sometimes on stage, pregnancy, either of which may reinforce sentiment in favour of them both.

238–303   *Portia's demand to have Brutus share his deepest thoughts with her proceeds by several stages, at each of which she puts forward a further basis for being treated as Brutus' equal. She skilfully rejects his evasions while exhibiting profound strength and love.*

238–57   While Portia makes clear that she is obedient as a Roman (or Elizabethan) wife was expected to be, mentioning that she left Brutus alone when he required it, her retort in her first line is sharp, and her catalogue of his clear symptoms of unease is direct and detailed. An Elizabethan audience would recognize the physical signs of someone in disturbed thought, matching Brutus' own account of himself at the start of the scene. Portia's concern for the effect on Brutus of this derangement of his nature is obviously the result of careful observation and deep affection. Both the love and the concern will be important in her portrayal, and also her determination, evident from her brief account, not to be put off with excuses.

258–71   Brutus may be brusque or tender in his excuses that he is not well, and it is possible he is consciously ironic when he says that he intends to embrace the means to regain his health: he may be thinking of the assassination, of a cure for Rome and them all. Portia, however, derides his excuses, pointing out their transparent insufficiency. She brushes them aside, makes clear she knows the 'sick offence' (l. 269) that troubles him must be in his mind, and declares that she, as his wife, has a right to know what it is he is thinking.

271–9   Portia probably pauses in hope of a response before strengthening her appeal by kneeling, thus changing the stage picture dramatically. Her speech becomes less directly demanding as she instead appeals by her beauty, by Brutus' love for her, and above all by the marriage vow that united them, that he share the weight on his mind. But her determination and intelligence are shown by the way she adds a further result of her observation: that she has seen the conspirators. The half line at the end of her speech may indicate a pause for Brutus to reply, or possibly he breaks in to complete the verse line before she can continue.

279–99   Brutus probably raises Portia as he says 'Kneel not', and this physical action reinforces his next speech in which he praises and acknowledges her as not only his 'true and honourable wife', but also as dear to him as his own heart's blood (ll. 289–91). The emotion of these lines is almost tangible, a great wave of love, admiration, and gentleness from Brutus. Nevertheless, Portia recognizes that this is no answer to her demand to know his inmost thoughts. Somehow, in performance, she has to demonstrate that her refusal to be put off is part and parcel of her love. Her language becomes stronger, almost sarcastic, as she implores him to recognize their marriage as partnership, not simply legalized prostitution (see p. 92).

Next, she counters the (unspoken) male expectation that a woman cannot keep a secret: with great pride she claims the men in her family – her famous Stoic father Cato, and Brutus himself – as testament to resolution beyond what is normally expected of women. It is already clear to the audience that she is a remarkable woman in her own right.

300–3   Portia's wound in the thigh is a final demonstration to Brutus of her worthiness to share his thoughts, a physical display of 'constancy' (l. 300), of her ability to keep a secret. The moment can be awkward to stage if its purpose is not understood. Its power derives directly from the earlier talk of the intimacy and partnership of marriage. Portia has chosen to wound her thigh precisely because of its proximity to the sexual organs; while there is nothing sexual about the wound, its intimate location means it must be kept hidden from all but her husband (except in some modern dress productions, where the passage is often cut). Portia has physically displayed her trust, and worthiness of trust, in their conjugal partnership.

303–10 Brutus is clearly overwhelmed by emotion at the cumulative evidence of Portia's love, devotion, constancy, and determination to share his thoughts. But a knocking at the door is a sharp interruption, and a return to a sense of events accelerating. Brutus is clearly sincere in his promise to share his secrets with Portia very soon (as we find out in II.iv), but now he urges her inside and once again turns his attention to business.

310 to the end That Ligarius is sick would have been evident to Shakespeare's audience from his headscarf ('kerchief', l. 316) as well as Lucius' announcement, and perhaps the casting of a cadaverous actor (see II.ii.111–13). In modern productions the actor must employ a 'feeble tongue' (l. 314) or physical frailty to convey weakness; use of crutches or a wheelchair risks undermining this when discarded at l. 322, since it may imply that the illness has been faked. That the illness is real gives point to the culmination of all the scene's references to sickness and health for both the individual and the body politic. And Ligarius throwing off his kerchief or other visual indication of sickness, and vowing to follow Brutus in whatever he plans, provides a new injection of energy and purpose into the end of the scene (see p. 91). He clearly suspects that assassination is in prospect; time is so pressing that they immediately exit (to Caesar's), even before Brutus has told him the details. The '*Thunder*' as they leave is probably a cue for the next scene, so rapid is the scene change.

Act II, scene ii

1–56   This first sequence, between Caesar and Calpurnia, has a number of parallels with the preceding sequence between Brutus and Portia, but also significant differences. It has two main sections, the division marked by the dramatic entry of the Servant at l. 37.

1–7   Whereas the storm was not in evidence in II.i, now Caesar enters amidst renewed thunder and lightning effects, recalling the turbulence of I.iii. His first line indicates his awareness that disturbance on earth may be linked to godly or cosmic upheaval. And whereas Brutus was dressed, Caesar enters '*in his nightgown*': this indicates prosaically that it is still night, but can also operate as an emblem of unreadiness in Caesar for whatever is to come. Much of the effect of the scene will depend on the acting of Caesar, who has a variety of options, especially around the question of superstition and fear. Is his decision to demand an immediate sacrifice by the augurers a direct result of the furious storm and Calpurnia's fearsome nightmare?

8–37   Calpurnia may have heard Caesar's instructions for sacrifice as she enters, but in any case she is driven by the fear for Caesar generated by her nightmares (l. 3), by the storm, and by reports of appalling portents seen during the night, including graves opening with their dead (as if it were the Day of Judgement), a battle in the heavens that 'drizzled blood upon the Capitol' (l. 21), and ghosts shrieking in the streets. It is no wonder that she says 'I do fear them' (l. 26). In *Hamlet*, Horatio recounts similar 'harbingers' of 'feared events' (I.i.106.14–.15), for the belief that 'heavens themselves blaze forth the death of princes' (l. 31) was widespread in both Roman and Elizabethan times (see pp. 102, 104). Calpurnia therefore urges Caesar not to go forth, first using the commanding 'You shall not' (l. 9), then trying to persuade him of the danger after such portents. Many different kinds of relationship between the two have been presented on stage, including a young trophy wife infatuated with the power of the older man, a loving woman deeply caring about her lifelong partner, a superstitious and hysterical neurotic scorned by an irritated politician, and a dipsomaniac Calpurnia repelled by Caesar's neglect and coldness. Caesar's responses to her, including his own third-person use of the emphatic 'shall' in 'Caesar shall forth' (l. 10), display an imperious sense of his own particularity. While his argument that portents apply to everyone equally is calm and reasoned, and his comments on the pointlessness of living in fear of death (again, compare *Hamlet*: 'If it be not now, yet it will come. The readiness is all', V.ii.159–60) may be thoughtful, his confidence is expressed as arrogance, and the actor may make Caesar look both boastful and unpleasant by turning the lines into bombast. In Plutarch, however, the context is positive; see p. 101.

37–56   The interruption by the Servant will be heightened if he is himself terrified of the absence of a heart (signifying courage) from the augurers' sacrificial beast. Perhaps the Servant hurriedly exits straight away. Calpurnia, too, may respond to the news with fear, so it is a question of stage interpretation whether Caesar's determination to ignore a potential threat is his standard response, a kind of role-play of his self-image in front of Calpurnia, or a real attempt to comfort her. Certainly the image of Caesar as more dangerous than Danger is overblown arrogance, and Calpurnia is quick to remark that his wisdom has been buried in overconfidence. Her offer of a face-saving solution – that he blame her fear for his not attending the Senate – is intensified by kneeling, just as Portia did, to her husband. Why and how does Caesar agree to her proposal? He may be overwhelmed by affection for his wife, as Brutus appeared to be for his. Or he may himself be genuinely afraid, and glad of an excuse not to go forth. But the way he places the responsibility on her ('for thy humour I will stay at home', l. 56) distances him from the decision almost as if he is blaming her. Perhaps he is patronizing her, or humouring her. The physical relationship between them as he raises her from her knees (if he does) will tell an audience as much as the words.

56–107   *This sequence, in which Decius persuades Caesar to attend the Senate after all, consists of three segments: Caesar instructing Decius to give the Senate no reason for his non-attendance; Decius flatteringly reversing Calpurnia's interpretation of her dream of the bloody statue; and Decius adducing additional reasons that lead to Caesar's reversal of his decision.*

56–72   The moment Decius Brutus appears, the scene ceases to be domestic, and Caesar henceforth largely ignores Calpurnia. Decius' elaborate greeting will remind the audience of his easy assurance at II.i.203–12 of his ability to flatter Caesar and fetch him to the Senate. The more overt Decius' flattery appears in the current scene, the weaker Caesar will appear. Caesar sounds anything but weak initially, however, as he refuses to send any excuse to the Senate for his intention to absent himself. A few moments earlier he was proposing to have Mark Antony say he was sick. Perhaps the change is because Decius is not so close a friend that Caesar feels uncomfortable with the white lie, or perhaps Caesar is simply playing to Decius. Calpurnia's ill-judged interjection certainly reinforces Caesar's determination to be seen always in the light of his carefully crafted image as a man of superhuman will; and it is the repeated word 'will', as both noun and verb, that dominates this segment of the scene: 'The cause is in my will; I will not come' (l. 71).

73–91 Caesar's shift from his usual hauteur to an engaging personal tone of affection with Decius may catch an audience by surprise, though it will recur later in the scene with the other conspirators. 'Because I love you' (l. 74) will remind an audience how little Decius loves him, and Caesar's open friendliness will offer a sharp contrast to the hypocrisy of those betraying him. His account of Calpurnia's dream of Caesar's statue spouting blood is a reminder of the importance of bloodletting as a Roman characteristic. Decius, perhaps after a shocked pause as he considers how to counter this unexpected resistance, or perhaps as smoothly as the rest of his oily performance, cleverly reinterprets the dream in what we would now call more Christian terms: the blood representing martyrdom, salvation, and princely reputation. Caesar is entirely persuaded, and the actor needs to consider how quickly and easily this happens.

92–107 As in Plutarch (see pp. 102–3), the final segment of Decius' persuasion is masterly in the way he appeals to Caesar's ambition by mentioning – as a certainty – that the Senate will offer him a crown, but might change their minds if he fails to attend. He instantly continues, thus pre-empting any possible high-minded declaration from Caesar about not caring about the crown, to suggest both potential mockery of Caesar for being henpecked, and even doubt about his courage. Decius is doing precisely what he said he would in I.iii, and presumably watches Caesar carefully during his speech to see if the lure is being taken. This may explain the short line at 101; Decius may see anger brewing in Caesar at any aspersion on his reputation or courage. Decius' obsequious declaration of his love and duty may be in order to calm Caesar, or to head off Calpurnia if she looks like interrupting. Caesar's final lines to Calpurnia may be serious, or cruel, or in jest, and her silent reaction will tell us much about him, and about her own foreboding. The Folio gives no exit direction, and it is possible that she exits at this point to see to the robe he requests, or she may stay and a servant exit (or Caesar may call to servants offstage). It is unlikely the robe is given to him at this point, since he would need to remove his nightgown first. If Calpurnia does stay on stage, her isolation may become increasingly apparent.

108 to the end The scene ends with a sequence in which Caesar greets all who have come to accompany him to the Senate: almost all of them, as the audience knows, conspirators who intend to betray him this very day. They may exchange glances with Decius to ascertain if Caesar will go forth. The entrance of Publius, whom Caesar greets first, will cause the audience to wonder who he is; although not seen in the play prior to this, perhaps he is not a conspirator (see III.i.85), but a well-wisher, just like Antony. Some productions have substituted Cassius, who intended to be present, for the unknown Publius, in which case the absence of greeting to Cassius alone is marked. Caesar's friendly acknowledgement of previous enmity with Ligarius shows us a new side of Caesar, not only trusting, but easy in acknowledging political difference while valuing friendly relations. Will this be played as sincere, like the magnanimous historical Caesar (see p. 101); or will Caesar simply appear a consummate politician? Or an unwitting victim?

Antony's separate entrance throws particular attention on him, including that of most of the conspirators who wish him dead too. And if Calpurnia exits at l. 118 or 119, her departure will leave Caesar without his last determined guardian against danger. The irony of Caesar's unwitting confidence while surrounded by treachery is foregrounded by two asides: Trebonius openly exulting at the murder being imminent, and Brutus, invited with the others to share wine with Caesar, and probably the last character left on stage, grieving for his friend even as he prepares to kill him.

Act II, scene iii

1 to the end   As the stage empties, the audience is left with anything but a clear-cut sense of whether the planned assassination will be the destruction of a tyrant by a band of patriots, or a dangerous act of treachery against established authority. Now the single unknown figure of Artemidorus reading over a scroll or letter he has written (in some productions, making minor corrections) reminds us that the issue is still in doubt; Caesar has admirers who will try to protect him. But Artemidorus is a sole figure, in contrast to the growing group of conspirators over the last few scenes, and he 'laments' the precarious state of 'virtue' (l. 12). Nevertheless, he has been able to identify all the conspirators. His direct address to the audience also tells them that the scene is now to be imagined as Caesar's route to the Capitol, and the final lines as he exits reinforce the suspense: events hang in the balance.

Act II, scene iv

1–20   Portia's agitation will be evident from her entry, perhaps quite fast, possibly overlapping with the exit of Artemidorus, and in the contrast between her distraction (her language very jerky in its rhythms) and the uncertainty of the young Lucius. Her agitation reflects supposed weakness of women's self-control ('constancy', l. 6), while her attempts to suppress any show of concern reflect Portia's 'man's mind' (l. 8). It is clear that Brutus has kept his promise to tell her of the conspiracy, and now she is burdened, as women so often are in wars or planned subversion, with deadly knowledge but no active role to play. Hence her over-receptive hearing, imagining she hears 'a fray' in the direction of the Capitol. There is potential for humour from Portia too, if she directs 'How hard it is for women to keep counsel!' (l. 9) to the audience, either as self-mockery, or as an ironic comment on men's assumptions. Lucius, too, may raise a laugh at l. 2 with his bewilderment at being given a useless errand. Although young, and with few lines, his observation of and response to Portia will be telling: he may be calm, or bewildered, or greatly concerned for her.

21–38   The 'feeble' (l. 36) Soothsayer presumably enters slowly, and approaches Portia slowly when she summons him. The contrast in physical rhythms will be striking, like that between her jerky verse and his calm and measured responses. Asking the time not only raises the suspense, but will also resonate with audience Biblical knowledge of 'the ninth hour' at the crucifixion (l. 23). Portia's anxious questioning elicits non-specific fears from the Soothsayer, who, like Artemidorus in the previous scene, demonstrates a degree of fatalism about whether Caesar will 'befriend himself' (l. 30) by taking heed of warnings. His words about danger, 'None that I know will be, much that I fear may chance' (l. 32), are printed as two lines in Folio; if delivered as such, the short lines may sound like his characteristic mode of warning. No doubt Portia's alarm at his intention to try to alert Caesar to dangers will be manifest as he departs.

39–46   Alone again (with Lucius), Portia suddenly realizes that 'the boy [may have] heard' (l. 42) the agonized worry she has just shared with the audience. This moment encapsulates the extraordinary doubleness of Shakespearean dramaturgy, one character sharing with the audience a fear about another character who gives no sign of knowing there is an audience. She covers up by saying to Lucius that 'Brutus hath a suit / That Caesar will not grant'); her next words, 'O, I grow faint' (ll. 42–3), may then be her sharing with the audience this example of the strain on her from the endless deceit, rather than simply an announcement (in Plutarch she does faint; see p. 93). Lucius, observing her agitation and faintness, may have to support her for a moment before he leaves to report her 'merry' to Brutus at the Capitol, while Portia resolutely exits in the opposite direction, as if into the house to wait.

ACT III

Act III, scene i

1 to the end *This, one of the two central scenes of the play, develops in three main movements: first Caesar's assassination, then the decisive involvement of Antony with the conspirators, and finally Antony's short section at the end in which he predicts and prepares for civil war.*

1–12 On the Elizabethan stage, as Portia and Lucius leave by opposite doors, and a trumpet sounds a 'Flourish', Caesar and his senatorial train almost certainly entered in splendour through the great central opening. Any additional actors who could be rounded up would provide a few lictors and additional senators. Only more modern productions can sometimes provide citizens as well. Folio's inclusion of Lepidus is textually odd, and in the theatre Ligarius, already identified in II.i and II.ii as a keen conspirator, often replaces him. Careful choreography is needed to have Caesar encounter the Soothsayer; in modern productions he (and Artemidorus) can enter from another direction, but at the Globe perhaps Caesar led a processional circuit of the stage, thereby allowing the Soothsayer, who may have entered last, to establish himself and be seen by Caesar. His response to Caesar's cheerful challenge (l. 2) sounds alarmingly prophetic (see p. 102), and Caesar may amplify this sense by his reaction.

If Caesar has paused, this gives Artemidorus his opportunity to urge his scroll ('this schedule', l. 3) on Caesar, and the audience will be well aware that Decius must be improvising with Trebonius' scroll in order to ensure the conspirators get Caesar's attention first. Cassius may push

Decius forward, recognizing a potential danger. The tension is briefly relieved when Caesar refuses on principle to respond to the urgency of Artemidorus: 'What touches us ourself shall be last served' (l. 8); but note the royal plural of 'us' balancing the noble disinterestedness. The conspirators bustle Artemidorus out of the way ('give place', l. 10), and in some productions Cassius has followed his speech by seizing and tearing up Artemidorus' scroll. If it is discarded without being read, it lies on the stage offering mute ironic testimony to the knife edge on which events are balanced as Cassius urges them all 'to the Capitol' (l. 12). If Cassius has read it, the audience will see his appalled recognition of how close they were to being betrayed.

13–30   The fluidity of Elizabethan stagecraft is clear here, as the location changes to the Capitol simply by means of a change in activity on stage. Caesar probably moves upstage to sit on a Roman *sella curulis* or an Elizabethan throne, denoting his supremacy in the Senate.

   Meanwhile, an unknown senator (identified a few lines later as Popilius Lena) draws attention to Cassius, at some distance from Caesar, by wishing their 'enterprise' well (l. 13). Cassius may respond coolly, or may be visibly alarmed. Since Popilius merely replies 'Fare you well' (l. 14), the audience will share Cassius' uncertainty about how much Popilius knows, and whether, if he does know of the conspiracy, he really does wish it may thrive. Brutus has been observing, and quickly joins Cassius. As they hurriedly assess the potential danger, they also observe the 'dumb show', the wordless little play-within-a-play, as Popilius talks to Caesar (see p. 93). Whereas Cassius is, as Plutarch says, 'half beside himself', Brutus reveals himself as calm and 'constant' (l. 22) in a crisis. Further observation shows Caesar relaxed, Antony removed by Trebonius, and Metellus Cimber approaching Caesar. As the conspirators station themselves for action, with Casca reminded to strike first, their nervousness or ruthlessness will heighten audience expectation of what is to come. Many eyes will be on Casca, an aspect the 1953 film develops effectively (see pp. 126–8).

31–75   Caesar opens the formal session of the Senate, his physical placement likely to underline his pre-eminence: perhaps standing, but at a higher level than the senators, or more likely seated on a raised throne while everyone else stands below him. His assumption of quasi-royal status is further emphasized by the third-person reference to 'his Senate' (l. 32).

Metellus starts the planned moves of the conspiracy, his language and body both obsequious as he makes an extravagantly deep bow that probably finishes with him on one knee. This 'base spaniel fawning' (l. 43) may or may not be a deliberate ploy, but it certainly provokes Caesar. He despises Metellus' flattery and subservience, and uses the occasion to declare himself above 'ordinary men' (l. 37). The actor must decide to what extent Caesar is really angry and offended, or seizing a formal occasion for political purposes, or even pitying and trying to educate Metellus. Does the audience admire Caesar's moral probity? If they see, rather, principally the arrogance of the man, the conspirators will seem more justified. (For the possibility that ll. 47–8 were originally even more arrogant, see pp. 7–9).

Metellus initiates a second phase of the action, in what may be a planned move, as he calls for other voices (in physical terms, other conspirators) to second him. The evidence of l. 75 ('Doth not Brutus bootless kneel?') implies that Brutus kneels now as he kisses Caesar's hand (the audience may think of Judas betraying Christ with a kiss), and is joined, literally at Caesar's 'foot' (l. 56), by Cassius. Both of them are physically emulating Metellus' actions, and also starting to surround Caesar. Caesar is astonished to see Brutus doing this ('What, Brutus?', l. 155). This is a short line, perhaps suggesting a pause for its significance to sink in. Caesar may even stand up at this point. His response is even stronger than in the previous speech, reacting with arrogance worthy of a tyrant. He turns inflexibility into a virtue; he is 'constant as the northern star' (l. 60), the only man on earth to be god-like in his constancy ('Wilt thou lift up Olympus?', l. 74). At the Globe he would probably have gestured at the canopy over the stage, 'this brave o'erhanging firmament, this majestical roof fretted with golden fire' (*Hamlet* Q2, II.ii.291–2), when he spoke of the stars, the 'unnumbered sparks' (l. 63). Again, the question for the actor is how sympathetic or otherwise he should make Caesar.

Finally, Cinna and Decius, and presumably the rest of the conspirators, surround an appalled and increasing outraged or baffled Caesar. Almost his last line indicates his love for Brutus; how can Decius or the others expect to achieve anything when Brutus is already kneeling before him, and even that gesture is 'bootless' (l. 75). Casca will have positioned himself behind Caesar, who is probably standing by now. The physical intensity of the choreography is overwhelming.

76–7 Nowhere in the play is the stage picture more important than in this central action of Caesar's death. The two lines of dialogue are simply Casca calling attention to his initiating movement, and Caesar addressing Brutus in the last moment before he dies.

All the meaning in between is carried by the action. This may be ritualized, as Brutus wished, sacrificing 'a dish fit for the gods' (II.i.174), or may be, as he feared, the butchery that Plutarch describes (see p. 103). The stage interpretation of Caesar's death has a profound effect on audience understanding of its significance, and on their attitude to Brutus and the conspirators. Is Caesar a passive victim, or does he fight back? Is Brutus forced into action by Cassius (see p. 111), or does he stand back until he delivers the final blow? Is the style realistic, perhaps a bloody confusion of blows, or is it overtly choreographed, even stylized? How much blood is used? And crucially, how much of it is on the conspirators, and how do they react? Are there pauses as the killing proceeds? Are parts in slow motion? Where does Caesar's body lie when he dies? What is implied by lighting, sound, and the use of stage space? Kemble in the nineteenth century had Caesar stagger down from his dais, receiving a stab from each conspirator in succession as he zigzagged back and forth across the stage between them, ending facing Brutus downstage for 'the most unkindest cut of all' (III.ii.180).

As Brutus delivers the *coup de grâce* he may be horrified at what he must do; he may turn his face aside as he stabs; he may embrace Caesar in love and death; he may hesitate, or back away; he may be determined, even clinical, though this is less common, and less productive of the sympathy he will need later in the play. Political principle has become immediate, brutal, and messy. Brutus may well give evidence of realizing at this moment that killing Caesar is wrong and all is lost; or that the killing was right, but all is lost anyway.

Caesar's *'Et tu, Brute?'* ('And [even] you, Brutus?') recognizes again the pre-eminence of Brutus; whether with astonishment, bitterness, resignation, or forgiveness is for the actor to decide. Similarly, the actor must decide whether 'Then fall, Caesar' (l. 77) means 'it is time to die if I have been so betrayed,' or 'my death must be deserved, if even Brutus judges thus.' He may well muffle his face in his mantle before he falls, as described by Antony at III.ii.181–6. This moment of tragic confrontation is overwhelming in its intensity.

78–95   Now that Caesar is dead the conspirators' sense of purpose is less clear. Staging may suggest confident patriots rejoicing at 'Liberty! Freedom!' because 'Tyranny is dead!' (l. 78); in the eighteenth century they crossed their swords aloft in a 'bush'. Modern productions are often

more ambiguous: the conspirators may initially be stunned, or looking
at the blood on their hands or togas. They may be uneasy. Despite the
cries of 'Liberty! Freedom!', Brutus is unsuccessful in urging the 'People
and Senators' to 'Fly not' (ll. 82–3), though it is not clear whether
they exit now or with the greybeard Publius at l. 95. Metellus urges the
conspirators to make a stand, in case they are attacked, whereas Brutus
seems to remain confident that they need only explain themselves and
all will be well. But talk of how they will 'abide this deed' (l. 94) may
suggest a premonition of catastrophe.

96–121   The stage has emptied of all but the conspirators. Cassius,
as always, has hair-trigger reactions: seeing Trebonius appear, his
anxiety about Antony instantly appears. Trebonius' report that all
the populace have reacted with consternation, 'As it were doomsday'
(l. 98), leads Brutus to thoughts of doom, as if accepting they may now
all die. His high stoicism becomes absurd, however, when he suggests
death was a gift they gave Caesar. Is he simply over-reacting to the
horror of the killing, or does he at this moment believe such sophistic
hyperbole? He avoids dwelling on this image, however, by plunging
on to demand that they all smear themselves in blood. Intended as a
noble ritual and tableau, one that will be echoed and 'acted over' (l. 112)
down the ages, the result may be otherwise (see pp. 1–2). Then they
start to exit in heroic (or horrific) procession, only to be halted by the
entry of an isolated and unknown servant.

122–46   Antony's servant not only kneels, but then throws himself
flat in a posture of utter humility before Brutus. He may be fearful and
overawed; he may be intensely aware of Caesar's corpse lying nearby,
and the bloody swords above him. Like a herald, however, he formally
repeats Antony's message of submission, to which Brutus responds, as
he did in II.i, that they do not seek Antony's death. The servant departs
with his master's safe-conduct assured. Cassius again makes clear his
unease about Antony, but does not challenge Brutus' authority. His
short line before Antony enters may signal a significant pause, or possibly
interruption.

147–253   *Antony's initial emergence as a major figure develops in three stages:
first, Brutus offers him peace and collaboration; second, Antony accepts, despite
his open grief for Caesar; third, Antony secures, against Cassius' resistance,*

permission to speak at Caesar's funeral. Dramatic interest in this section is vested
principally in what Antony, a largely unknown quantity to the audience, will do.

147–83   Antony has been only a minor figure up to this point in the
play. Now his entrance and his speech place him as the dominant character on stage, and a major counterforce to Brutus and the conspirators. One character entering to a group always stands out, and there are
many possible ways to play it. Antony may keep his focus on the dead
Caesar initially, ignoring the conspirators and baulking them of the
acknowledgement they will expect. The conspirators may have to fall
back to allow Antony to get through. What Antony does determines
what is to come, and his action seems to rob Brutus and his companions of the initiative. While Antony may have an element of political
deliberation in what he does, his most powerful effect is likely to stem
from deeply felt emotion and grief for Caesar.

After his first three lines Antony addresses the conspirators (perhaps standing after having knelt by the body, or fallen prostrate upon
it), and again his words are unexpected. Far from being deferential, he
declares himself ready for death, since the conspirators' swords have
been ennobled by Caesar's blood; this is a historical moment not to be
repeated. Antony's words and emotion provide, for the first time, both
human grief for his friend, and a reminder of the mighty Julius Caesar
whose pre-eminence has indeed lasted much more than 'a thousand
years' (l. 159).

Brutus is driven to explain himself to Antony, almost seeking his
pardon, and Cassius' very different approach, offering political influence, is alike in that Antony is invited to join them. Brutus invites
Antony to 'be patient' (l. 179) until they have time, and then Brutus will
justify his action. Both Brutus and Cassius having made their offers,
they and the rest of the conspirators must wait for Antony's decision
and reply. In this short section since Antony entered he has secured the
initiative. Despite the shared line 183, he may well take his time before
replying, thus reinforcing his centrality in the scene.

183–226   Antony draws out his apparent acceptance of friendship
with the conspirators in several stages. In a striding stage image he
deliberately takes Brutus and then each of the others in turn by the
bloody hand, thus literally sealing amity (or displaying its impossibil-
ity) in Caesar's blood. He controls the physical action, advancing to
each man in turn, or requiring each in turn to approach his proffered

hand. The prefatory comment to Brutus, 'I doubt not of your wisdom' (l. 183), may be simple reassurance, or may convey at least to the audience a heavy irony, as perhaps earlier when he referred to the conspirators as 'The choice and master spirits of this age' (l. 163). Similarly, his greeting of 'valiant Casca' (l. 188; for the man who struck Caesar from 'behind . . . on the neck' (V.i.44–5)) and 'good Trebonius' (l. 189; for the man who lured him away during the assassination) are carefully chosen. Antony is playing a part to Brutus and the rest, and is likely by now to allow the audience to know this, at least in part.

Probably returning to a dominant stage position to address the conspirators, Antony audaciously pre-empts their obvious suspicion of him, which may be evident in their body language. He acknowledges the 'slippery ground' – perhaps literally so, with stage blood, as well as metaphorically – of appearing either 'a coward or a flatterer' (ll. 191–3). Then he makes another unexpected move: he returns to his deeply emotional eulogy of Caesar, conjuring the 'spirit' of Caesar (l. 195) to witness the inappropriateness of his 'Shaking the bloody fingers of thy foes' (l. 198). Antony's language is as 'purpled' (l. 158) as Caesar's toga and blood, a rhetoric that Antony can use both to heighten his real anguish and to express, by the contrast between the excessive poeticism of his words and the brutal stage image of bloody hands and swords around a corpse, his real distance from alliance with Brutus.

Cassius, not Brutus, is the man who changes the register of the language. Cassius, whose belief that Antony should be killed may still be evident, presents a political ultimatum: are you with us or not?

Antony's reaffirmation of his friendship is accompanied by an apparently casual proviso: that they give him reasons 'Why . . . Caesar was dangerous' (l. 222). Significantly, Brutus steps in (perhaps physically) to reply in place of Cassius, and to once again assure Antony that their reasons would satisfy even a 'son of Caesar' (l. 225). The actor of Brutus will need to decide how much he allows it to be evident that Brutus has an unfailing expectation that reasonableness is all that is needed in human affairs. Has he missed the depth of Antony's emotion just as he has failed to hear the ironies?

227–53 Antony's securing of his final request, like his request for reasons for Caesar's death, sounds like an afterthought, especially after completing Brutus' last line with 'That's all I seek' (l. 226). Is Antony elaborately casual, or does it seem to be the second in the pair of provisos? Either way, the request may well provoke a sharp physical

indication of negative reaction from Cassius. In some productions
Brutus has to physically restrain Cassius from attacking Antony with
the sword he still carries.

When Brutus readily agrees to Antony's request, Cassius instantly
moves Brutus away in order to spell out the danger (see p. 94). Cassius
again displays his nervous agitation, as at the start of the scene and
earlier in the play. Brutus' words 'By your pardon' (l. 235) seem likely to
be an interruption, cutting Cassius off in full flow. Brutus follows the
pattern of II.i in calmly and reasonably offering his reasons for contra-
dicting Cassius, and in arrogating to himself the right to make the final
decision. Cassius is not persuaded, however, and his line 'I know not
what may fall. I like it not' (l. 243), which may be to Brutus, or may be
to the audience after Brutus has turned back to Antony, provides the
audience with further reason to be alert to the question of whether or
not Antony is sincere.

Finally, Brutus presents Antony, rather formally, with the terms
under which he may take Caesar's body and speak at the funeral.
Antony's quick half-line acceptance, 'I do desire no more' (l. 253) is not
completed. Perhaps Brutus and the others pause, expecting him to
say more. If so, Brutus' final line before the conspirators leave may be
slightly anti-climactic, thus once again giving Antony dominance.

254–75   Mark Antony is left alone on the stage with Caesar's corpse,
and for the first time can speak what is in his mind. In an extraordinary rising tide of grief, love, and anger the rhythms build irresistibly
throughout this bravura speech.

The first couplet starts quietly with Antony, perhaps kneeling again
by Caesar, seeking forgiveness for his apparent collaboration with the
conspirators, but by the time he spits out 'these butchers' in the second
line (l. 255) his anger is clear. He observes his own hand, bloody from
shaking those of the conspirators, as he declares enmity to the hand
that actually shed the blood.

Then at l. 259 he starts to prophesy 'Over thy wounds' – he is still
near Caesar's body – civil war, the most vicious of all kinds of war.
As the rhythms build he paints a devastating picture of a society torn
apart, and habitual brutality so deadening all human pity that 'moth-
ers shall but smile' (l. 267) when their babies are torn apart in front of
their eyes. Caesar's spirit is invoked, 'ranging for revenge' (l. 270), with
Atè, the classical embodiment of strife and lawlessness, as his ally.
Caesar, now with 'a monarch's voice' (a clue to the actor of Antony

about the climax of this speech), will let slip famine, sword, and fire: 'the dogs of war' (ll. 272–3). Although the speech must appear spontaneous, the breathing, vocal control, and intellectual structuring require immense acting skills. It is like an aria in opera. And the actor must decide the balance between controlled authority and passionate outpouring; between anger and grief; between pleasure and dismay at what he is predicting and will himself instigate.

The final couplet, following 'the dogs of war', seems to slow down, the language imitating the groans of dying men, the human misery that civil war always leaves in its wake. It allows Antony to come down from the extremity of crying 'Havoc!' (l. 273) in a mighty voice; he may return to Caesar, and the image of a body 'groaning for burial' (l. 275).

276 to the end The 'dangerous Rome' (l. 288) may be emphasized by a defensive movement from Antony as the servant enters, before he identifies him as serving Octavius Caesar. The servant has barely given his message of Octavius' imminent arrival before he sees Caesar's body. His reaction is personal and human, the first time the audience has seen a non-political response to Caesar's death. The servant's tears for Caesar are eloquent, and may induce greater sympathy for Antony. But Antony does not give him long. He quickly instructs the servant to tell Octavius to delay until Rome is less dangerous, then suddenly changes his mind. The actor can show us Antony thinking on his feet, the decision being made, that the servant should be retained until after the funeral. Antony reveals his plan to test how the populace of Rome will react; then he can send more specific plans to Octavius. In effect, the second half of the play is being put in train. The presence of the servant is also useful to help remove Caesar's body from the stage without the indignity Hamlet has to impose on Polonius when he has no help to 'lug the guts' (III.iv.186).

Act III, scene ii

1 to the end *The Forum scene has three main movements, punctuated by two descents from the 'public chair' (l. 63): Brutus satisfies the plebeians about the assassination of Caesar; then Antony arouses their pity; and finally Antony incites them to violence against the conspirators.*

1–11 The plebeians from I.i enter, perhaps following Brutus and Cassius, demanding reasons for why Caesar has been killed. If Brutus and Cassius are still bloodstained from III.i it will be clear how quickly events are developing. The plebeians are hugely important in this scene. How many are there? Have they a unified purpose, or are they a collection of individuals? How angry are they at this first entrance? How easy is it for Brutus to split them, and send some away to listen to Cassius? Certainly the First and Second Plebeians seem prepared to listen, and their brief comments allow time for Brutus to ascend (see l. 11). On the Globe stage it is possible he went offstage to reappear on the gallery, but more likely that he mounted a raised dais or platform on the main stage, to represent the classical 'pulpit' or 'public chair' (see p. 94), perhaps the same one that Caesar had used in III.i.

12–39 Brutus may gain some sympathy if he has to struggle to be heard at first, but the speech is sober, rational, and, significantly, in prose. This calm reliance on reason repeats what the audience by now expects of Brutus. Nevertheless, the speech is carefully structured, with a series of balanced antitheses. The actor of Brutus will have to decide whether this is calculated rhetoric, or if this is in effect Brutus' credo. Is he flattering the plebeians, or does he actually trust their ability to 'Censure' and 'judge' (ll. 16, 17)? Will he sound as if he really does weep for Caesar's love of him, rejoice at Caesar's good fortune, and honour his valour? When Brutus invites any friend of Caesar he has offended to speak, having already condemned any such man beforehand as 'vile' (l. 31) and unpatriotic, is this rhetorical skill or Brutus' deep belief in Rome? The plebeians' reply, that he has offended 'None, Brutus, none' (l. 34), will, if enthusiastic, tend to reinforce audience respect for Brutus' strict Roman principles and integrity.

40–61 The entry of Antony with Caesar's body interrupts Brutus' speech. What is the manner of the disruption? Antony may ensure the attention is on him, or he may have Caesar's body the focus. Caesar may in death have 'official' state attendants such as lictors and soldiers, or the followers may be few and anonymous. In modern productions the press may cause a commotion. The time taken for the entry will influence whether Brutus is forced to allow a long pause before he resumes.

Brutus stresses that Antony, although not one of the patriots who slew Caesar, is nevertheless welcome. And certainly Brutus has the crowd's attention as he holds aloft his still-bloody dagger to announce that he too is willing to die if ever Rome shall pass judgement on him. He may be emotional or calm.

As Brutus descends to the main stage it is clear that he has satisfied the plebeians. Their enthusiasm carries heavy irony, however: 'Let him be Caesar' (l. 50). It is unlikely Brutus hears this, but the audience will. The crowd has really not understood Brutus at all – it wishes to crown the man who killed Caesar to prevent any kingship in Rome. Brutus leaves entirely alone, honourably urging the plebeians to listen to Antony. The audience sees departing a Brutus they may admire, but whose political judgement they will by now be doubting.

62–72 This is the start of the second major section of the scene, in which Antony moves the plebeians to pity of Caesar, as described in Plutarch (see p. 104). They are thoroughly engaged in what is going on, and actively comment. They urge the 'Noble Antony' to ascend to the 'public chair' (ll. 63–4) just as Brutus did, but their threat to anyone criticizing Brutus, and their approval of Caesar's death, make clear the potential hostility Antony will face. At l. 72 crowd noise prevents Antony from making himself heard; often in modern productions the crowd is massively hostile for some time, thus making Antony seem more impressive when he ultimately wins it over (see pp. 112–13). Most often the crowd will be facing Brutus and Antony as they speak, with their backs to the audience, but other arrangements are possible. Sometimes the theatre audience itself is in effect part (occasionally all) of the crowd. Directors will decide whether they wish the focus to be more on the orators, on the interaction between orator and crowd, or even in a few cases on the crowd as the protagonist of the scene. Affecting this will be such decisions as how much light is on the crowd, and how much realism the plebeians are asked to bring to their acting. Is the crowd full of individuals, each with a separate point of view? Or is it a single dark, impersonal beast? Do the plebeians stand still to listen, or do they attract attention by constant movement?

73–107 Antony's now-famous opening lines are often drowned out by the crowd in modern productions, but they are equally effective even if the crowd is silent. Antony's assurance that he has not come to praise Caesar (though this is precisely what Brutus, at l. 58, said he should do) is clear evidence of his awareness that the plebeians are hostile. He is therefore gradual in his approach, but early on sows two seeds that he will repeatedly return to: that 'Brutus / Hath told you Caesar was ambitious', and that 'Brutus is an honourable man' (l. 77–8, 82). In a series of examples Antony offers his own experience of Caesar – loyal as a friend, augmenting Rome's finances, pitying the poor, refusing a crown at the Lupercal – and each time juxtaposes the evidence against Brutus' bare statement, and Brutus' honour. The pattern of syllogisms invites refutation of the second premise: that Brutus is indeed honourable. But the pattern of the verse lines provides a less dense sense of argumentation than in Brutus' prose speech, and therefore greater possibility for alternative readings.

How soon the undermining of Brutus becomes apparent to the plebeians, and to the audience, will therefore vary from production to production. Sometimes Antony seems to show his hand too soon, provoking crowd anger, and he has to retreat and downplay any tendency to sarcasm and manipulation. In other productions he will seem genuinely respectful of Brutus, and puzzled at the apparent contradictions, thereby seeming to allow the plebeians to reach their conclusion before he does. But the relentless repetition of 'honourable man' does its work.

Whatever the interpretation, the reaction of the plebeians is vital, and Antony is likely to be gauging it carefully. His outburst of human emotion, condemning the crowd's refusal to mourn Caesar, and announcing that he is so overcome that he must 'pause' (l. 107) till he regains his composure, therefore presents a crucial choice to the actor. He can play Antony as really overcome with grief, exactly as he says. Or he can make it clear to the audience that this is as much a calculated ploy as his rhetoric, the deliberate creation of an opportunity to take stock of crowd reaction (as Brando does in the 1953 film; see p. 127). Or he can do both: display genuine grief, but also an ability to employ his own real emotion to political effect.

108–17   As Antony pauses, the plebeians below him offer comment. Although their reaction is mixed, the majority are sympathetic to Antony, and willing to be persuaded (all too easily) that Caesar was not ambitious. Antony, if he can hear these comments, may allow the audience to sense his response, and it may now anticipate a stronger anti-Brutus element in his speech.

118–27   Antony does start more overtly to rouse the mob's passions, first by directing everyone's gaze again to the dead Caesar, then by mentioning for the first time the possibility of raising them to 'mutiny and rage' (l. 122). The irony with which he labels the conspirators as 'honourable' becomes heavier and more evident, as does his rhetorical declaration that he prefers to wrong the dead (i.e. Caesar), himself, and them rather than the 'honourable men' (l. 127).

128–52 Just as Antony a few moments earlier used Caesar's body as a visual and physical aid to what he was saying, now he electrifies the plebeians by producing another physical object: a 'parchment' (l. 128), which he says is Caesar's will. And having displayed the will, he immediately frustrates the curiosity he has aroused by saying he does not intend to read it. He further inflames their desire to hear it by saying that its contents would make them regard Caesar as a holy martyr, any tiniest relic of whom would become treasured forever. His pause after the half line at 137 creates a vacuum, as it were, which is quickly filled by the plebeians crying out that he should read the will. Indeed, their use of 'shall' at l. 148 constitutes a demand, no longer a request.

Antony's rhetorical performance has successfully cast the plebeians now as the active party, and Antony as their servant. Thus he can paint his reluctance to read the will as an unwillingness to 'inflame' them (l. 144), and a fear of wronging 'the honourable men / Whose daggers have stabbed Caesar' (ll. 151–2). Clearly he is sufficiently sure of himself now to address directly the facts of Caesar's assassination, stabbed to death by Brutus and the other conspirators. And, still holding Caesar's will in his hand, he is inviting the mob to assure him of their new attitude to the conspirators. The temperature of the scene is rising fast.

153–65 Whereas Brutus descended from the pulpit because he had said all he wished to say, and evidently did not hear (or ignored) the comments of the crowd, Antony hears exactly what he wants to before he, too, descends. He hears a vehement condemnation of the 'honourable men' as 'traitors' and 'villains, murderers' (ll. 153–5); and he hears renewed and repeated demands that he should read the will. The mob's intensity here will demonstrate how extraordinarily successful Antony's manipulation of them has been. His skill is further shown by his seeking their permission to descend, emphasizing the rhetorical pretence of being their servant.

Antony urges the crowd to move, to make a ring about the body of Caesar, and he descends onto the main stage to be amongst them and next to Caesar. These two major movements: the plebeians moving to new stage space, surrounding Caesar more closely, and Antony descending from his higher level to their level, serve as a visual marker of a changed dynamic in the scene and the play.

166–93   Antony begins the third and final section of the scene on a
quiet note, probably aided by dead silence from the crowd. Indeed, part
of Antony's skill so far has been his ability to vary the mood and tempo
of what is a much longer public address than that of Brutus. Now he
recalls a summer evening after a great Roman victory (and reaction
from the plebeians can help indicate how famous Caesar's achievement
was). And, as he did with the will, he holds a physical object on display
to enforce focus and particularize his speech with repeated demands to
'Look', 'See', and 'Mark' the various rents in the fabric of Caesar's mantle. The catalogue of traitorous wounds increases the tempo and anger
again, leading to 'the most unkindest cut of all' (l. 180), that of Caesar's
'well-belovèd' (l. 173) friend Brutus. Antony's imagery of Caesar's blood
flowing out to investigate whether it is really Brutus acting so 'unkindly' –
i.e. both cruelly and unnaturally – is emotive and elaborate, and probably acts as a springboard for a great rush of energy from Antony.

Antony describes Caesar's death as resulting even more from the
treachery of Brutus than from the wounds. Antony is likely to be at full
volume as he then moves from the personal and specific to the general-
ity of treason: 'Then I, and you, and all of us fell down, / Whilst bloody
treason flourished over us' (ll. 188–9). The plebeians' weeping may be
quiet or audible, and again Antony allows a moment of quiet sentiment –
but only for a couple of lines. Then he snatches them into renewed
energy and anger as he declares he can show them more.

193–202   'Look you here!' (l. 193) cries Antony as he caps his use of
the will and the mantle by now displaying the bloody body itself. The
'piteous spectacle' (l. 195) may include the image of Antony weeping
over Caesar, but more likely Antony's gaze will challenge the plebeians. Their reaction is immediate and overwhelming, committed to the
'mutiny and rage' (l. 122) that Antony earlier disclaimed. The audience
will see an angry mob aroused, shouting, enraged, probably danger-
ously out of control. The harder they make it for Antony to get them to
pause and listen to him again, the more dangerous they will appear.

203–25   Antony has brought the mob to the boil, but now he deliberately delays them from 'mutiny' (l. 205), a word that also ends this
speech (l. 223) as a renewed provocation. The actor of Antony will
decide whether or how much he may allow the plebeians to see that he
is pretending to disclaim violence. The nature of crowd reaction and
interjection will also have a bearing on this. His reference to the 'wise

and honourable' (l. 207) conspirators is likely to draw jeers, whether he uses heavy irony or appears entirely disingenuous. If the latter, it is easier for him to portray himself as the 'plain, blunt man' (l. 211) that the audience knows he is not. His rhetoric is as skilful in this speech as his disclaiming of it is a pose. And this reversal allows him to posit a Brutus who would incite them to mutiny. Thus by the end of a speech that started quietly he has once again reminded the plebeians of who their target is, and renewed their sense that they are in charge (since he is, he says, too weak an orator to influence them). And as at the end of his last long speech, the result is another surge of anger, and perhaps the start of a flow offstage to seek the conspirators.

226–52 For the second time Antony calls back the mob, perhaps with even more difficulty, depending on noise, mob mentality, or the start of plebeians leaving to hunt down the conspirators. This time, to reinforce their attachment to the Caesarian cause, he pulls another rabbit out of the hat: he reminds them of the will, and again waves it aloft. The audience will be well aware of the skill of Antony's manipulation of the mob by now. As in Plutarch (see p. 94), Caesar's legacy to the people of Rome is considerable: the reaction to the news of seventy-five drachmas to every citizen is 'O royal Caesar' (l. 237), with 'royal' indicating both munificence and monarchical status. Furthermore, Antony announces a vast area of public gardens to be created as a perpetual legacy. By the time he gets to 'Here was a Caesar! When comes such another?' (l. 245), Antony will probably need to be shrieking to make himself heard over the mob tumult; and he will be aware that he is now letting slip the dogs of civil war as he intended.

The plebeians will by now be in a frenzy, having been held back and further incited by Antony twice. They pour offstage with Caesar's body to cremate it, and from that fire to light the literal and metaphorical torches with which they will burn out the conspirators.

253–4 Antony is again left alone on stage, as in III.i when the conspirators left, a still focus after the tumult of his oration. His satisfaction will be clear, and so will be the exaltation from the adrenalin rush as much as from his astonishing success against all the odds.

254 to the end Again, the structure mirrors III.i. A servant enters (perhaps hesitantly) to find Antony alone on stage, and bring him news of Octavius. The Folio simply says '*Enter Servant*'. The Humphreys edition identifies this servant as Antony's, but it seems far more likely that he is Octavius' servant with whom Antony spoke at the end of III.i. Either way, his function is to bring news of Octavius' arrival in Rome, already ensconced with Lepidus at Caesar's house. Antony's reaction continues the exaltation of spirits seen a few lines earlier: 'Fortune is merry' (l. 259), he says. His joy is added to by the news of Brutus and Cassius having fled Rome in mad haste. Events seem to be tumbling over each other, and Antony is probably more than mildly self-congratulatory as he observes in the last line of the scene how successful he has been in stirring the mob to action. The audience receives no sense of Antony having any qualms about the havoc he has unleashed; on the contrary, Antony glories in simple triumph and power. Some at least in the audience, however, may have some foreboding about the suffering that is clearly to come.

Act III, scene iii

1 to the end This short scene was usually cut in the eighteenth and nineteenth centuries, but in the twentieth century, from Welles's production on (see pp. 116–17), it has often been of central significance in performance. It is often played as a night scene, which is entirely appropriate to a single figure being surrounded by an unpredictable and violent gang. But the word 'tonight' (l. 1) here carries an Elizabethan sense of 'last night', so the scene can be played as daytime, following on immediately from the plebeians rushing forth at the end of III.ii (see pp. 94–5).

1–4 After the tumult of the last two major scenes, a lone unidentified character enters. He answers the unspoken audience curiosity with direct address, telling them about his unlucky dream of feasting with Caesar (a pleasant dream heralds bad luck). His clothing may suggest an intellectual, perhaps physically slight or weak in contrast to the plebeians who are about to enter. In addition, he says he does not know why he has come outside, so his physical carriage and movement will reflect this lack of purpose.

5–27 The plebeians probably enter only at this point, their speed of entry overtaking Cinna the poet, or perhaps from an opposite door, thus blocking his way. There may be more than the four identified speakers, but even four thugs intent on random violence can be threatening enough; it becomes clear that they are simply looking for an excuse to do harm. The 'bang' (l. 18) Cinna is promised may be delivered instantly, and explain the brevity of his answers from then on. For although the answer about being a bachelor is a joke, and the other answers are satisfactorily neutral or pro-Caesar, the wit of his initial formulation, structured on the plebeians' list of adverbs – 'directly and briefly, wisely and truly' (l. 15) – may spark an anti-intellectual resentment in the mob.

28 to the end Cinna the poet is an innocent bystander who happens to share a common name with Cinna the conspirator. But his immediate clarification 'I am Cinna the poet! . . . I am not Cinna the conspirator' (ll. 29–32) carries no weight with the frenzied mob. Any excuse will do: 'bad verses' (l. 30), or an unacceptable name. 'Tear him' (l. 35) is a cry of blood-lust, and Cinna the poet will be torn to death. This may happen offstage if the plebeians force Cinna off with them, or it may happen on stage. If on stage, then the exit of the mob to look for more victims and destruction may see them dragging the body with them; or, especially when modern productions have an interval at this point, the body may remain on stage for a while as mute testimony to the results of inciting mob violence.

Whatever the staging of this scene, its emotional and intellectual force is clear. The audience sees for itself the irrationality and violence of the Roman citizens upon whose judgement Brutus was so reliant. And the audience sees precisely the price of the political rhetoric at which Antony has so displayed his skill.

ACT IV

Act IV, scene i

1 to the end   *Some critics and directors regard this, the last scene in Rome, as the end of the first half of the play; others, with some justification, see it as the beginning of the second half, the struggle between Antony and Octavius on one hand and Brutus and Cassius on the other. In modern productions the placing of the interval before or after (often for reasons to do with changing the stage setting) may be crucial in how the audience will think of the play's dynamic at this point.*

Entry stage direction   If the triumvirate have seated themselves, perhaps around a table, the cold-blooded ruthlessness of their business meeting to purge political enemies will be emphasized. If they are all standing, perhaps in a hurry, a sense of their responding to immediate danger may be greater. Costume will also be important: the young Octavius is often played in armour, ready for the campaign, as may be Lepidus, with Antony more relaxed and still in toga or other civilian wear. Antony has a list or scroll of names, and a pin with which they may be 'pricked' (l. 1) for death.

1–11   Shakespeare follows Plutarch (see p. 105) in showing all three men as equally callous in their agreement on who should be proscribed, Lepidus here trading the death of his brother for that of Antony's nephew. This can be acted as a testing of Antony, and Lepidus may also take time for silent consideration of whether to challenge Antony's sending him to fetch Caesar's will (so as cynically to reduce Caesar's legacies, so generously offered by Antony in III.ii). Tension between Octavius and Antony may also be evident, since actors and directors often like to treat their relationship as a prequel to their hostility in *Antony and Cleopatra*.

12–40   The moment Lepidus has left, Antony sounds out Octavius about dropping him from the triumvirate. Is this the older and more powerful Antony positioning himself to become the senior partner? Octavius is not deferential, however, and may even be hostile as he points to Antony's willingness to give Lepidus an equal voice in the proscriptions. Again at 'You may do your will' (l. 27) Octavius seems to reveal both pragmatism and a cool distancing of himself from Antony; this may be in effect a major character note for his performance. Antony seems not to notice, instead offering the younger man analogies of asses and horses at deliberate length, language quite unlike the quicksilver oratory of the Forum scene.

40 to the end   Narrative speed picks up again as Antony reveals that Brutus and Cassius are levying armies, and urges the need for a council to deal with the threat. Octavius is even brisker in agreeing, noting not only the danger from without, but also, as Hamlet would, 'That one may smile and smile and be a villain' (*Hamlet*, I.v.109). They are surrounded by danger, not least from false friends.

Act IV, scene ii

1 to the end   Usually called the Quarrel Scene because the argument and subsequent reconciliation between Brutus and Cassius occupy the main action, and a great feature of the play in performance from the time of the earliest performances (see p. 7), this scene is the longest in the play. It has three main structural elements: first the quarrel and reconciliation, then the council of war, and finally the appearance of Caesar's ghost to Brutus. Note that many editions of Julius Caesar *number a new scene, IV.iii, from l. 53, because the setting changes to Brutus' tent at that point.*

Entry stage direction   A drum offstage forewarns the audience of the entry of an army. In the Folio, the rest of the entry direction reads: '*Enter Brutus, Lucilius, and the army. Titinius and Pindarus meet them.*' Probably they are all in military costume, except perhaps the freed bondman Pindarus. The sense of two groups entering from opposite sides and meeting is confirmed by Brutus calling a halt to his army, and Lucilius relaying the order. Then Brutus greets Pindarus, who has arrived as a forerunner of Cassius. However, slight confusion can arise when it becomes clear in the dialogue that Lucilius has himself just returned from an embassy to Cassius for Brutus, and introduces Pindarus as if they had arrived together. And Titinius, an important friend of Cassius, is never greeted.

Two options are available. First, assume that Shakespeare knew that no-one in the audience would be occupied with the minutiae of realism. Lucilius is with Brutus as his lieutenant, and explains the situation; in performance this is very unlikely to cause confusion. (On the Globe stage, Lucilius would, like Pindarus and Titinius, probably have been wearing boots and spurs, signalling recent arrival.) Alternatively, assume that Shakespeare left some minor loose ends here, perhaps from not having fully decided at this stage the precise functions he wanted the new characters (such as Lucilius, Pindarus, and Titinius) to serve. In this case there are a number of stage solutions a director can impose in search of perfect logic. Either way the main point is clear: Brutus is in the field with his army, and a meeting – even a confrontation – is imminent.

1–13   With many new characters appearing, the audience will tend to place them initially by costume and function (military officer, servant, etc.), but also by their attitudes to Brutus and Cassius. Here, when Pindarus approaches, Brutus is as always courteous to a subordinate, though entirely straightforward about his dissatisfaction with Cassius. Pindarus replies politely, but with entire loyalty to his 'noble master' (l. 11).

13–30 As Brutus leads Lucilius apart from Pindarus and Titinius on the one hand, and the soldiers on the other, it is clear the trust he reposes in his lieutenant. Lucilius' report of the slightly cool reception he had from Cassius is balanced, and seems perceptive in noting aspects of behaviour that Brutus may wish to know about. Clearly Brutus has been concerned about Cassius, and this may have been evident since the start of the scene. The way in which he elaborates on 'a hot friend cooling' (l. 19) suggests that Lucilius is merely confirming what he already suspected, and the entire speech sounds more in sorrow than in anger. Just as everything in the scene up to this point, both stage picture and dialogue, builds anticipation of the meeting to come, so too does the sound of a '*Low march within*' (l. 24.1); the quiet backstage drum heralds the approach of Cassius' army, although Brutus seems not to hear it until l. 30 ('Hark, he is arrived'), a moment before Cassius enters.

31–52 The stage spectacle as Cassius enters is striking: Brutus has his army 'March gently on' (l. 31), presumably so that when each army halts (Stand, ho!'; ll. 32, 33) and the drums cease they will be symmetrically placed on stage. As the orders to halt are passed back by the officers the audience will see the full resources of the theatre company on stage: the armies in uniform, the soldiers (at the Globe) probably carrying long pikes, with eagles or battle standards aloft; and the two leaders facing each other at the front. Surprisingly, given what has gone before, it is Cassius who launches an angry attack on Brutus. Brutus is no doubt surprised, and his habitual calm 'sober form' (l. 40) seems to infuriate the volatile Cassius more, so much so that Brutus interrupts him at l. 41 to urge that they hide any show of dissension from their troops, and retire to Brutus' tent. There, says Brutus, he will give Cassius 'audience' (l. 46). Brutus may intend simply to say that he will listen to Cassius' grievances, but 'give you audience' is a phrase that implies inequality, and Cassius may well react to it. His instructions to Pindarus are curt, as he perhaps restrains his anger with difficulty. Brutus also orders his army to retire, and seems sufficiently aware of a likely explosion from Cassius that he carefully orders that no-one should approach his tent, and that it should be guarded by his own boy Lucius and one of Cassius' closest followers.

53–60 The shift into Brutus' tent at this point, like the shift from the street to the Capitol after III.i.12, needed no scenic change at all on the Elizabethan stage, only a willing imaginative collaboration from the audience. The placing of a table at this point, ready for the tapers that will be needed from l. 207.1, and perhaps Lucius' lute (see ll. 289–90) and the cushions that Varro and Claudius are later told to sleep upon (see ll. 292–300), can assist the sense of a private space. In the modern theatre, scenery and lighting may be more elaborate, especially if a new scene is thought of as starting here (see headnote to this scene), but the essential remains: the two men are alone in private.

Cassius' grievance is that Brutus has publicly condemned one of Cassius' officers for taking bribes, and ignored Cassius' letters on his officer's behalf (see p. 95). To Brutus' comment that he should not have supported a corrupt officer, Cassius retorts that in war they cannot afford to be overly scrupulous. As this dissension flares between the allies and friends, the audience may sense Caesar's spirit at work.

61–116 Brutus now goes on the offensive, and it is noteworthy that most of the longer speeches during the quarrel are his. He starts by accusing Cassius of accepting bribes, of having 'an itching palm' (l. 62). When Cassius says that only Brutus' noble name protects him from death, Brutus responds that Cassius' noble name is sheltering corruption from punishment. He declares, somewhat naively given what the audience knows of the lack of idealism in all but Brutus, that they struck Caesar down 'for justice' sake' (l. 71). He adds that Caesar was merely 'supporting robbers' (l. 75), not actively corrupt himself. This presents a dilemma for the actor of Brutus: since Brutus said nothing in II.i of Caesar 'supporting robbers', is he now adding a new reason for the assassination that he simply forgot before, or is he now rewriting history in order to justify himself?

There are other major questions for both actors. The emotional dynamic of the quarrel is as important as the content of what they say, and they must control the variety, contrast, and tempo as carefully as two musicians playing a duet. Brutus may rely on the stoic self-control that so infuriates Cassius; or he may, given what Cassius says later, for once lose his calmness and display uninhibited rage. Cassius is much more volatile as a character, and needs to decide on his pattern of anger, petulance, and perhaps self-pity. Any given production will have explored the options in rehearsal, and there are many, many possible ways for them to play against each other. Movement or stillness around the stage will be important, as will the treatment of properties: papers scattered onto the floor, chairs overturned, etc.

As Brutus gives a contemptuous gesture on 'graspèd thus' (l. 78), and says he would rather be a 'dog' than 'such a Roman' (ll. 79–80), Cassius replies 'bait not me' (l. 80), picking up the 'dog' reference – meaning 'don't snarl and snap at me as if I were chained to a post in a bear-baiting pit.' This seems to imply unusual anger in Brutus. He rejects outright Cassius' claim to be the more experienced soldier, provoking Cassius to a direct threat: 'Have mind upon your health. Tempt me no farther' (l. 88). The threat may be serious, or may be rash, unconsidered anger. Either way, Brutus' scorn mounts ('Away, slight man!'; l. 89), as does his anger ('Hear me, for I will speak'; l. 90). He seems to match Cassius in force, and presumably volume, ferocity, and perhaps, unusually for Brutus, movement. Berating Cassius for his 'rash choler' (l. 91), he adds insult to injury by refusing even to take the anger seriously; he claims that he will regard Cassius as a clown, an object 'for my laughter' (l. 101).

This may mark the high-water mark of Brutus' anger. If so, he might perhaps sit down after Cassius' despairing line 'Is it come to this?' (l. 102). The tone might become more deflated and exhausted, though the anger might rebuild at some points later. On the other hand, Brutus' anger may continue unabated here; it may not burn itself out until l. 116, or even l. 158, where 'Sheathe your dagger' makes it unequivocal. Certainly Brutus continues to taunt Cassius about being a better soldier, but at this point Cassius starts to back off, claiming to have said 'an elder soldier, not a better' (l. 108). When Brutus remains disdainful, however, Cassius is driven to threaten again: 'I may do that I shall be sorry for' (l. 116). In performance this may be accompanied by Cassius drawing or half-drawing his sword or dagger, a moment of high tension (see p. 7).

117–43 Brutus' response is disdainful of Cassius' threat: 'You have done that you should be sorry for' (l. 117). He may simply refer to the extortion, or perhaps he hints that Cassius killed Caesar for the wrong reasons. Certainly the *gravitas* of Brutus gives him the moral high ground, and brushes aside the physical threat from Cassius.

As this section continues, two main options face the actor of Brutus. The first choice is to continue to stress the moral authority and ethical integrity of Brutus. He ignores Cassius' threats, both verbal and physical, because he is committed to what is right. He declares bribery and extortion totally unacceptable. And he says he has always been generous with money to his friends, and would certainly not have refused Cassius. When Cassius responds that Brutus is too critical of a friend, Brutus replies that only a flatterer would allow friendship to obscure objectivity. This performance option, giving full weight to the moral stature that has made Brutus the acknowledged leader of the conspiracy, will tend to lend a heroic stature to Brutus.

An alternative, darker, reading is also possible. Brutus can be made to sound somewhat priggish, arrogant, even Caesarish, as he announces that Cassius' threats pass him by like 'the idle wind, / Which I respect not' (ll. 120–1), or when he invokes 'high Olympus' (l. 143) as a comparison for Cassius' faults. Movement, gesture, and attitude could reinforce this. More significantly, Brutus may allow the weakness of his moral argument to be sensed, for although he is unwilling to employ extortion to raise money, he is perfectly prepared to accept corruptly obtained money from Cassius. Playing the scene this way will tend to stress the inherent weakness and insufficiency of Brutus as a leader, and the inevitable downfall that must follow.

Does Brutus retain his fierce anger still, or is he majestically calm? Or a mix of the two? Finally, does Cassius let the audience see that his blaming of the messenger for the misunderstanding is a conscious evasion, very similar to that of Hotspur's refusal of prisoners in *Henry IV, Part 1*, I.iii.28–68?

144–58 Cassius, ignoring the substantive issues of corruption raised by Brutus, launches into a passionate explosion of grief and despair that his love for Brutus is not reciprocated. The audience may perceive this as a moving personal plea from a character who wears his heart on his sleeve, or as evasive self-pity, depending on how it is played. Cassius invites Antony and Octavius to revenge themselves on him, since his life is not worth living without the respect and love of Brutus. As he bares his breast and offers his dagger to Brutus to cut his heart (his love) out, he may well kneel, as Richard III does to Anne with the same offer in different circumstances in *Richard III*, I.ii.162–84. When Cassius claims that Brutus loved Caesar more, even when killing him, than he has ever loved Cassius, the audience will note whether and how Brutus reacts. The moment is likely to be held briefly, since the stage picture will be a visual summation of the quarrel. In Plutarch, 'they both fell a-weeping' (see p. 95).

158–74 Brutus may have abandoned the vehemence of his anger earlier, after l. 102 or l. 116, or may have maintained its energy until this point. When he says 'Sheathe your dagger' (l. 158), it is unquestionable that his 'fire' is 'cold again' (ll. 162, 164). This sheathing of the dagger marks the beginning of the reconciliation between the two men that will be confirmed by their shaking hands (ll. 168–9) and perhaps embracing. As Cassius reveals, perhaps unconsciously, that being 'but mirth and laughter' (l. 165) hurt him most, Brutus acknowledges that he was 'ill-tempered' (l. 167). By the end of this section the reconciliation is complete, possibly with both men laughing at Brutus' promise to imagine any future anger from Cassius as really his mother chiding. A quiet intimacy prevails after the severe tension of the quarrel.

175–92 Shakespeare avoids melodrama by not having an unknown peacemaker burst past Lucilius and Titinius into the tent at the height of the quarrel, but just as the reconciliation is complete. The newcomer's admirable purpose is therefore redundant and slightly comic, especially when he quotes a well-known couplet from Homer (ll. 181–2). Cassius laughs at him (the printed 'Ha, ha!' at l. 183 being effectively a stage direction for laughter), and it is only the combination of the couplet and Cassius' reference to 'rhyme' that will give the audience a clue that the ridiculous 'Cynic' (philosopher) is a would-be poet (l. 183). Brutus, however, is angry – an emotionally compelling deflection of the emotion of the quarrel by both men onto the luckless Poet. Sometimes Brutus chases him away or beats him. The Poet in effect earths or grounds the energy accumulated during the quarrel, and his exit leaves the air cleared as Brutus and Cassius prepare for a council of war, and send young Lucius (who may have come on stage behind the Poet, or may be called to offstage) for wine.

193–212 Now the two men are alone again the emotional temperature is lower. When Cassius reproves Brutus for a lack of philosophy, he may be light and jesting. Brutus' response is, by contrast, devastating: 'Portia is dead' (l. 297). Only now do Cassius and the audience suddenly become aware of the strain Brutus has been under, and they will apprehend the quarrel with new understanding. Of course the actor will have known this all along, and suppressing the personal grief of Brutus will have been part of the subtext of his performance of Roman 'formal constancy' (II.i.228). That Portia committed suicide by swallowing hot coals intensifies the shock, and Cassius' ejaculation 'O ye immortal gods!' (l. 207) sums up the impotence of anyone faced with such horror.

Reaction to both Portia's death and Brutus' extraordinary stoicism is extended by having Lucius enter at this moment with candles, which signal that night has fallen (in modern productions the lighting may have become very gloomy, and now brightens), and with wine. The shared bowl of wine follows the sheathed sword and the handshake as finally sealing the reconciliation between Brutus and Cassius, as well as being an unspoken acknowledgement of their grief at Portia's death.

213-30 When Titinius and Messala enter for the council of war they may be accompanied by Lucilius, who was included in the orders at ll. 189-92. As they all sit, presumably about a table with a candle, Cassius continues to utter his concern for Portia. Brutus quietly cuts him off, but the audience will be aware of the immense control Brutus must be employing to put duty ahead of personal grief. Brutus and Messala each refer to letters they hold confirming that Octavius and Antony are approaching with 'a mighty power . . . toward Philippi' (ll. 219-20). Perhaps Marsalla then hesitates, leading Brutus to prompt him, 'With what addition' (l. 222). Only then does Marsalla report the brutal proscriptions in Rome, including Cicero, a name famous even to audiences two thousand years later. Cassius reacts, as he did earlier to news of Portia's death, to the human and individual loss. And perhaps Marsalla hesitates again.

231-45 This section, a second account of Portia's death, is thought by some critics to have been intended for deletion by Shakespeare (see p. 9), and sometimes cut by directors. It can be powerful in performance, however, and if it is played the actor of Messala will presumably allow his uncertainty and concern about the content of his letter to show as he asks Brutus if he has news of Portia. He evidently hopes to avoid being the one to break the news, and even denies having any. But Brutus not only senses his evasion, but rejects the opportunity to evade the issue himself, simply saying 'tell me true' (l. 237). Brutus' calm reception of the news impresses Messala as an example of Roman philosophy, but will impress the audience even more as evidence of Brutus' fortitude in grief. Cassius, whose nerves are closer to the surface, admits in an aside to Brutus that he has as much philosophy as Brutus, but cannot imagine bearing the burden with such constancy. Thus both Cicero and Portia act in this section as harbingers of tragedy.

246–75 The council of war now reaches its decisive stage. Brutus proposes that they march to Philippi (which, the play implies, is much closer to them than to the enemy) immediately, and invites their views. Cassius is the only one to differ, or to comment at all, but in performance Titinius and Messala (and Lucilius if present) may share looks of unease, may even make it clear that Cassius is their spokesman, if they, like Cassius, immediately recognize the military weakness of what Brutus proposes. Cassius emphasizes that his advice is the opposite: "Tis better that the enemy seek *us*' (l. 249; my emphasis).

Brutus offers what he says are better reasons, though in fact weaker. More significantly, when Cassius wishes to debate ('Hear me, good brother – '; l. 262), Brutus simply interrupts and overrides him. It may start to seem in performance that Brutus has a consuming wish and psychological need, as in Plutarch (see p. 96), to provoke a single decisive battle so that things will be decided one way or the other. Brutus' movement from reasons to aphorisms ('There is a tide in the affairs of men'; l. 268) will tend to shift audience focus away from his weak military strategy and towards the human dilemma, or even heroism, of seizing Fortune by the forelock (an equivalent to taking the tide 'at the flood'; l. 269). The audience may not know yet how wrong Brutus is, but may remember his mistake in underestimating Antony earlier in the play. And, again, shared glances between the other officers present may give the audience a clue about their judgement.

Why, then, does Cassius defer to Brutus yet again? Perhaps because of the emotional aftermath of the quarrel, and Cassius' deep need for Brutus' affection? Or perhaps resignation, knowing that Brutus is not open to debate, but that he is essential as leader of their cause. Either way, or even if both are operative, the council of war ends with agreement to 'meet them at Philippi' (l. 275).

276–88 This short transition as they all rise from the council of war is an opportunity for Cassius and the other officers to reinforce our impression of Brutus. Cassius, especially, emphasizes his love for Brutus, and his deep concern about their quarrel, just as Brutus singles out

'Noble, noble Cassius' (l. 282). The emotion engendered by the quarrel is still in the air, and the only 'division' (l. 285) recalled is the quarrel, not military tactics. Reconciliation is the mood as they all take their farewells of Brutus and depart to sleep. Lucius waits, holding Brutus' 'gown' (ll. 286, 289), in modern terms a warm dressing gown.

289–317 'Give me the gown' (l. 289) says Brutus, but this is not preparation to sleep, but for a quiet time for writing or reading (see p. 96). And he asks Lucius to get his instrument, probably a lute. Then follow two examples of why his subordinates are so attached to Brutus. He summons two of his men to sleep 'on cushions in my tent' (l. 293), but they immediately say that they will stay awake in case needed. Brutus, however, insists they sleep, in case they are not needed. Similarly with young Lucius, whom Brutus has already noted is tired (as in II.i), his master in effect apologizes (surprisingly, in Elizabethan terms) for blaming his servant for losing his book, and for asking him to play music when he is tired. Lucius does play and sing '*Music, and a song*' (l. 316.1), and Brutus may sit at the table again to listen.

The mood of this section is perhaps more important than the action. A quiet, domestic harmony is established by gentle language and 'sleepy' music, and by the lack of any immediate objective for Brutus other than relaxation. Whether or not this will raise audience anticipation of disruption is uncertain, though modern lighting and sound effects have sometimes been used to counter the serenity of the scene as written.

316.1–17 We have no knowledge of what '*Music*' and '*song*' (l. 316.1) might have been intended or even written by Shakespeare. He may have left the decision to the musicians, since any 'sleepy tune' (l. 317) will serve the purpose. Sometimes in production Lucius only plays, realist critics and directors feeling it unnatural to have someone fall asleep during or immediately after singing, but audiences attuned to Shakespearean dramaturgy find no difficulty with both. The duration of the music may extend this section of the play significantly.

317–24 Sleep descends swiftly on Lucius, in the middle of a line, leaving Brutus to contemplate on the similarity between sleep and death. Continuing his considerate behaviour, he crosses the stage to take the lute from the sleeping boy, then sits at the table to get the benefit of the candle in order to read. (The benefit would have been symbolic on the Globe stage, but modern productions are usually more realistic in dimming the rest of the lights.) The movement back to the table and candle, and the attention given to the book will draw audience attention closely to him alone.

324.1–25   'How ill this taper burns' (l. 325) exclaims Brutus, ensuring audience focus on him and the candle, focus that in modern productions is likely to be enhanced by the rest of the lights being very dim, and perhaps the candle appearing to burn a supernatural blue (see *Richard III*, V.v.134). With audience attention on Brutus, the appearance of '*the Ghost of Caesar*' can be sudden and unexpected, as implied by Brutus' 'Ha! Who comes here?' (l. 325). However the 'monstrous' (l. 327) appearance of the Ghost is achieved, its sudden entry (whether by trap door, from the darkness, or, in modern productions, sometimes by projection, eerie amplified voice, image of the constant 'northern star' (III. i.60), huge statue, or other means) will be the more startling if Lucius, Varro, and Claudius do now cry out fearfully in their sleep as Brutus later claims. Although the Ghost does not identify itself as Caesar, the stage direction does, so it is likely that the audience will know immediately who Brutus' 'evil spirit' (l. 332) is. Brutus confirms at V.v.17 that he saw 'The ghost of Caesar'.

325–38   As in *Hamlet* (Shakespeare's next tragedy), the Ghost may be 'a spirit of health or goblin damned' (*Hamlet*, I.iv.21), 'some angel, or some devil' (l. 329). Brutus is uncertain if indeed it is an entity, a 'thing' (l. 328), at all. It is 'monstrous' (l. 327; and see p. 96). It makes his blood run cold and his hair stand on end. Even with the technical effects available for a sceptical modern audience, the acting of Brutus rather than the appearance of the Ghost will be the primary avenue for a sense of how dreadful and abnormal the 'apparition' (l. 327) is. Although he is aware it could be a conjuration of his own imagination (see l. 326), he does, like Hamlet, challenge it to speak, an act that must appear to take great courage. Whether Brutus is composed or fearful, approaching the Ghost or distancing himself, will be acting and production decisions.

   The Ghost announces itself as Brutus' 'evil spirit' (l. 332); that is, the ghost of the murdered Caesar intent on revenge. Brutus is remarkably brave to be talking to it at all, and shifts from the simple futurity of 'I shall see thee again?' to the emphatic 'I will see thee . . . then' (ll. 334–6).

And having gained the courage to question it further (again like Hamlet), he finds it has vanished (perhaps by a trap door, or in modern productions veiled by darkness, dry ice, or other technical means). It leaves behind the echo of 'at Philippi', which occurs three times in four lines, ominous and prophetic. And all the time the three figures sleeping on stage have slept on.

339 to the end As Brutus calls the others to wake up, Lucius is still half asleep; but while Brutus explains this away (perhaps jokingly) to the audience, he does not notice that Lucius' dream is of the strings being 'false' (l. 341). In effect Lucius has had a nightmare of his instrument being out of tune, which the audience may associate with the Ghost, especially if Lucius appears distressed. Similarly, the reaction of Varro and Claudius to Brutus' agitation may add powerfully to the effect of the Ghost having dislocated matters. All three deny any knowledge of having cried out; the audience will know whether they did or not, and this also will have a bearing on how the audience reacts to the supernatural powers of the Ghost. A new day approaches (usually assisted by stage lighting in modern productions), and Brutus sets the armies on the move towards, as the Ghost has reminded him, Philippi.

ACT V

Act V, scene i

1–12 As in IV.ii, an offstage or possibly on stage drum will herald the entry of two generals with their army, complete with eagle standards. Octavius may share with Antony his exultation that Brutus and Cassius have abandoned the high ground and descended to Philippi to do battle; or, given his coldness at ll. 18–20, his attitude here may be simply cool and critical of Antony for having been mistaken. Either way, his comments confirm what the audience probably suspects already: that Brutus was militarily inept in overriding Cassius' advice at IV.ii.248–52. Antony sounds relaxed, claiming that he knows the enemy's thoughts and plans. They would prefer not to fight, he says, but are descending with 'fearful bravery' (l. 10; probably meaning 'a rich display of armour and weapons in order to cause fear' – cf. 'fearful' at I.iii.78) simply to give the impression of courage.

12–20 The Messenger rushes on in the middle of a verse line, and an immediate exit would reinforce the urgency of his report that the enemy is advancing to do battle. At this critical moment Octavius flatly refuses to accept the left wing as Antony instructs, but says he will take the traditional honour of leading the right wing. He also refuses even to discuss it. Shakespeare has carefully transferred Plutarch's report of disagreement between Brutus and Cassius to Antony and Octavius (see p. 96). This dissension between the two triumvirs has a long stage tradition of being played to the hilt, partly in anticipation of *Antony and Cleopatra*.

20.1–26 A drummer probably enters beating a march as Brutus, Cassius, their lieutenants and army take the stage facing their opponents. In addition to weapons and eagle standards, they may carry the scarlet heraldic military coat that is the Roman 'sign of battle' (l. 14; and see p. 97). The symmetry of their stage confrontation is matched by the paired speeches from each side as they anticipate a parley. Despite Octavius' insistence at ll. 18–20 on taking precedence in battle, here he defers to the older Antony as to whether they should fight immediately or exchange words. Nevertheless, it is Octavius who instructs an officer to await the signal for battle.

27–48 The battle of verbal insults that precedes the real battle is structured like a debate, a taunt from one side being answered by a retort from the other. This first section is also clearly built around the difference between 'Words' and 'blows' (l. 27). The initial sallies from Brutus sound calm, and may be delivered with his typical courtesy; but there is potential for sarcasm, and even for mock-pedantry towards Octavius, as if he is so young he needs to be taught (l. 29). Antony responds for both of them, sneering that Brutus treacherously offered 'good words' even as he killed Caesar with 'bad strokes' (l. 30). The exchange becomes more heated as both Brutus and Cassius remind Antony of his hypocritical expression of friendship for them with his honeyed words. Finally Antony is driven to fierce and direct accusation of the conspirators for the violence with which they 'Hacked' (l. 41) Caesar even as they 'bowed like bondmen' and 'flatterers' (ll. 43, 45). Cassius' response to this verbal and emotional onslaught is not back to Antony, but to remind Brutus, either in sorrow or in anger, that Brutus rejected his advice that they assassinate Antony too. If these words are a quick aside to Brutus, they need not break the emotional tension between the

two sets of leaders; if aloud so the others hear, then the additional com-
plication of words between Cassius and Brutus may provoke Octavius,
who has from the start favoured fighting rather than talking.

49–66 Octavius interrupts the traditional battle of insults among
the three older men with a demand that they get on with the real battle. He draws his sword to add visual impact to his words as he swears
to avenge Caesar's death, or himself become another victim called
'Caesar' (l. 54) to the conspirators' swords. By calling them 'traitors' (l. 55)
he emphasizes that the trading of insults is really a battle for the moral
high ground, and Brutus responds by claiming for himself the title
of 'honourable' (l. 60), which he can do on the basis of defending the
Republic. After a final sneer from both Cassius and Brutus, Octavius
seizes the initiative again by calling Antony away, throwing defiance at
their opponents, and leading his army offstage 'to the field' (l. 66). He
has, during all his time on stage since the start of the scene, demonstrated an ability to unbalance both his ally Antony and his enemies;
and the audience will be intrigued by a surprisingly strong and independent character of whom they have seen little up to now.

67–92 Cassius' storm imagery of the impending battle (ll. 67–8) continues the high sense of energy in the scene, and is probably followed
immediately by a spatial rearrangement enabling Brutus and Cassius
to occupy the entire stage. Then Brutus calls Lucilius forth from the
army, and Cassius calls Messala. Although it is clear that Brutus and
Lucilius confer aside while Cassius and Messala occupy audience attention, the Folio stage direction – *Lucilius and Messala stand forth* – implies
more attention to symmetry and less to realistic motivation than do
most modern productions and texts.

Following Plutarch closely (see pp. 96–7), Shakespeare has Cassius
impress upon Brutus' friend Messala his misgivings about their military strategy, reminding him of how Pompey was forced into the same
position (against Caesar), and lost. Cassius' sense of foreboding is reinforced by his new willingness to consider ill omens, in this case the
army's abandonment by a pair of lucky eagles, and their replacement
by a 'canopy' (l. 88) of birds of carrion. The intimacy of Cassius' revela-
tions to Messala, as he stands beside him and takes his hand, is in sharp
contrast to the formality of the public exchange of insults between the
two armies that has immediately preceded this sequence, and leads
the audience into the realm of the personal. Cassius then recovers his

spirits and energy, ready 'to meet all perils very constantly' (l. 92). (This seems a more likely option, given his typical emotional volatility, than a calculated decision as a commander to pretend to resolution he does not feel.)

93 to the end The audience has just experienced the tension between Antony and Octavius, the verbal sparring between the two sides, and the quieter but anxious revelation by Cassius to Messala of his misgivings about the forthcoming decisive battle. Now, as Brutus dismisses Lucilius (who, with Messala, no doubt now leaves the two leaders alone), the mood of the scene changes to one of united friendship and harmony, although the imminence of the battle informs the scene as the soldiers observe their leaders' final discussion and await the order to advance (see p. 97). Cassius expresses a hope for success and a peaceful old age, but prepares for 'the worst that may befall' (l. 97), acknowledging that defeat will probably mean death for one or both. In response to Cassius' question about how Brutus will face defeat, Brutus replies that he'll stick to his philosophical opposition to suicide. He criticized his father-in-law Cato for his famous suicide when Caesar overcame Pompey, and now reasserts the Platonic and Stoic view that his duty is to endure all 'with patience' (l. 106). When Cassius shifts from abstract philosophy to the prospect of being led 'in triumph' (l. 109; cf. I.i.31–51) as a shamed captive, Brutus strongly rejects the idea that he might ever 'go bound to Rome' (l. 112). In other words, despite his philosophy, he would commit suicide, that most Roman of deaths.

As they take what they both clearly expect to be an 'everlasting farewell' (l. 116). Brutus recalls the Ides of March as the inciting incident that has led them here. For the audience, the constant reminders of Caesar do not distract from Brutus and Cassius, but they do keep the famous name central to the significance of the action to come. As Cassius echoes the words of Brutus' farewell the two men may well embrace. In at least one production, when Cassius said they might yet 'smile indeed' (l. 121), the actor astounded the audience by producing his only smile of the play.

Brutus in his final speech of the scene regathers the stage energy by initiating their movement to battle. 'Come, ho, away!' (l. 126) is almost certainly a loud command, quite possibly followed by the command being repeated by the officers as the army moves off. The drummer may start beating the '*Alarum*' required by the following stage direction (see next note).

Act V, scene ii

Entry stage direction The '*Alarum*' is the distinctive drumbeat, recognizable to Elizabethan audiences, that calls soldiers to arms (Italian *all' arme!*), and on the stage signals a battle atmosphere of conflict and confusion. The rest of the play is punctuated by alarums, and in performance this constant noise of battle (which in modern productions often includes automatic gunfire reinforced with lighting effects) gives an effect of heavy fighting all around from which characters briefly seek respite and confer. The immediate re-entry of Brutus and Messala straight after their exit is unusual, but will in part be covered by the time it will have taken their soldiers to follow them offstage at the end of V.i. If Brutus is, in performance, accompanied by Lucilius and other officers, the leadership will be emphasized, but the urgency and personal responsibility lessened.

1 to the end This very short scene is one of intense urgency, as the five imperatives in six lines to 'ride' (ll. 1, 6) make clear. Brutus intends to seize the moment and attack Octavius without delay, and clearly much depends on his messages that the commanders of the other wing should follow suit. An audience is unlikely to notice that if Octavius really led his right wing, as Shakespeare indicates in V.i, he would be facing his enemies' left wing under Cassius, for, as Plutarch confirms (see pp. 97–8), Brutus led the forces on the right. The '*Loud alarum*' called for in the midst of Brutus' speech would be a most unusual addition to the urgency; it is more likely a Folio misreading of '*Low alarum*', indicating fighting at some distance.

Act V, scene iii

1–8 The stage direction '*Alarums*' may in performance be accompanied by '*excursions*' (soldiers issuing forth to fight briefly, often ending with one side pursuing the other offstage), thereby giving visual immediacy to Cassius' cry to Titinius to observe how 'the villains fly' (l. 1; referring to his own troops; see p. 98). Since the dead body of the cowardly ensign-bearer Cassius has killed seems to be gestured at 'here' (l. 3), somehow the ensign must get on stage and die. The scenario Cassius describes – his troops fleeing from Antony's, and Cassius slaying the ensign and seizing his standard – may have been enacted during an excursion before the first line, leaving Cassius standing holding the ensign, with the dead officer at his feet. ('Ensign' can mean both the standard and the standard-bearer). Titinius bewails the way Brutus' unwise impetuosity has left Cassius' wing of the army surrounded by Antony's troops.

9–33 Pindarus (whose costume may indicate his status as a slave) enters with repeated urgent injunctions to Cassius to 'fly further off' (l. 9) because Antony has captured his camp. Cassius, however, does not panic; he decides to stay where he is, and instantly sends Titinius to verify whether a formation of troops he sees 'are friend or enemy' (l. 18). The excitement of a battle in which advantage and danger shift every moment is conjured by the words and uncertainty. Cassius' weak eyesight adds to the uncertainty, and he sends Pindarus 'higher on that hill' (l. 20) to observe Titinius and the unknown troops. The 'hill' was probably the upper balcony level of the Globe, since Pindarus calls from '*above*' at l. 26, but it could have been from a stage 'rock' (cf. V.v.1), or can be entirely imaginary, like, presumably, 'This hill' at l. 12. While Pindarus ascends, the tone shifts profoundly: Cassius addresses the audience in deep meditation, making clear his sense that this will be his last day of life. Then we are abruptly returned to the action as Pindarus reports on Titinius apparently fleeing enemy horsemen, but then being captured. An offstage '*Shout*' (l. 32) of triumph seems to confirm this disaster. Then the tone shifts again as Cassius flatly tells Pindarus to descend.

34–50 Cassius, alone and typically volatile in his emotions, condemns himself for outliving the friend he has sent to his death. The audience will see and hear in his attitude the culmination of all his premonitions of disaster. When Pindarus re-enters a moment later, Cassius reminds him of his bond to do anything he is ordered, and demands he kill him. In the text, it is clear that Cassius hands Pindarus the sword, covers his face (with his cloak, according to Plutarch; see p. 98), and then is stabbed by Pindarus. Historically, many productions have preferred to emphasize the nobility of Cassius by having him kill himself. Either way, of course, it is suicide; and either way, Cassius recognizes that Caesar is revenged with the same sword with which he was himself killed in Rome.

Pindarus has been freed from slavery, but he laments the death of his master (possibly physically, crying or on his knees, as well as verbally) – an important emotional signifier as the audience reacts to this sudden death. Pindarus then runs from the stage to 'Where never Roman shall take note of him' (l. 50). And although most of this act has one sequence following quickly on the last, productions often hold a momentary pause here. The audience considers a bare stage and the dead Cassius: both politically and humanly the implications are profound.

51–79   The entry of Titinius wearing a victory garland (probably of laurel or oak leaves) with Messala indicates that Cassius' suicide has been a tragic error. As Messala explains the success Brutus has had, they discover Cassius dead. Both men realize that suicide following misconception of the progress of the battle is the cause, and both lament Cassius with admiration and affection. Titinius evokes a blood-red sunset as not just the end of 'Cassius' day', but also of Rome as they have known it – of Republican Rome. And Messala generalizes from Cassius' pessimism to the wider effects of Error itself, personified as the child of Melancholy (l. 67). The tone is elegiac but deeply depressed. Then, as Titinius casts about for Pindarus, Messala leaves to take the unwelcome news to Brutus.

80–90   Titinius, left alone with the dead Cassius, shifts into the second person singular of intimate friends. He rehearses the warm greeting from the friendly troops, the shouts that, ironically, Pindarus and Cassius did hear but, as Titinius says, misunderstood. 'Alas, thou hast misconstrued everything' (l. 84), he laments. The warmth of devotion that Cassius can inspire may come as a surprise to the audience, a late revelation of further complexity in the characters of the play, and an emotional response. Two stage actions now reinforce that sense. First, Titinius removes his garland and, as desired by Brutus, places it on Cassius' brows. The irony and pathos that Cassius is already dead is matched by our awareness of how painful the news will be to Brutus, but also balanced by the image of Cassius triumphant despite his defeat. Second, Titinius takes Cassius' sword – already seen in I.iii, in III.i, in IV.ii, and moments earlier when Cassius died – and acts 'a Roman's part' (l. 89) by committing suicide with it. Now the sword that killed Caesar has killed two of his enemies, and again the stage is silent, bearing only the dead.

91–110   As the '*Alarum*' (l. 90.2) maintains the noise of continuing battle, Brutus enters with not only his lieutenant Lucilius, and Messala, but also with four new unnamed military men. This is typical of this late stage of the play: evidence of support, loyalty, admiration, and affection from a large number of almost anonymous characters. The dead Cassius and Titinius are clearly at some distance from the point of entry onto the stage of Brutus and his officers, but as they approach the dead men Brutus realizes, presumably with shock and anguish, that Titinius is not in a posture of mourning. Young Cato, who must have run ahead at this point, confirms that he is dead.

Brutus' eulogy for Cassius starts by invoking, as Cassius did (ll. 45–6), the spirit of Caesar which is mighty even after death, leading the conspirators to kill themselves. Even the *'Low alarums'* (l. 96) may imply Caesar's ghost stalking the battlefield. Brutus, of course, accepted earlier that he would encounter Caesar again 'at Philippi' (IV.ii.333–4), so there may be an element of reflectiveness in this speech. Cassius, crowned with a garland, the loyal Titinius beside him or even partly on him, lies dead in front of Brutus and the audience, a subject for regard as 'The last of all the Romans' (l. 99). In saying that Rome will never breed Cassius' equal, Brutus is acknowledging the irrevocable change in Roman politics brought about by the life and death of Caesar as well as praising Cassius as unmatchable (see p. 99). As earlier in the play, Brutus lets us see his own deep emotion under stern control. Only in one line does he address Cassius directly ('I shall find time, Cassius, I shall find time', l. 103), with a promise to make time to mourn him as he wishes. Given their various disagreements throughout the play, and Cassius' less elevated motives for the assassination, Brutus' expression of loss and love may be surprising and deeply moving.

Brutus now briskly prepares for the 'second battle' (as Plutarch calls it), identifying for the first time three of his companions by name: Labeo, Flavius, and most importantly 'young Cato' (l. 107; see next note). Since Antony in the following scene makes no mention of Cassius, it is probable that the two bodies are now removed, which may in itself add to the elegiac tone of the entire segment.

Act V, scene iv

Entry stage direction–1.1   The Folio text requires only a further off-stage *'Alarum'* at the start of the scene, which may imply that initially Brutus is, like a good general, rallying his followers during a brief lull in the battle. If so, he probably leaves in one direction to renew battle while Young Cato and Lucilius prepare to seek it in another direction.

However, editors and directors often specify renewed fighting on stage as Brutus enters, which then gives many options about how the next few moments may unfold. The key element at the start is that Brutus is encouraging his troops prior to an exit (whether after l. 1 or during the general fighting at l. 6.1) to continue the battle bravely. If Brutus is beset by Antony's soldiers, that will open the possibility of Cato and Lucilius acting to relieve pressure on him (see next note).

2–15 Young Cato's brave and daring (or boastful and foolish) proclamation of his famous name (his father was remembered as a Republican martyr; and see II.i.296), and Lucilius' claim to be Brutus, may both be based on Plutarch's description of them trying to relieve pressure on Brutus (see p. 99). On stage they may dynamically distract some of Antony's soldiers from pursuing Brutus, in effect sacrificing themselves for him. This individual heroism may appear chivalrous or merely foolhardy and pointless, since the stage action has Antony's soldiers as a group killing Young Cato and capturing Lucilius. Lucilius seems to have stopped fighting for a moment to mourn Young Cato, and is possibly captured from behind. A squad of soldiers overcomes individual officers. Lucilius' invitation (either by offering money or simply by claiming to be Brutus) for the soldiers to kill him reinforces the audience's sense of his loyalty to Brutus. And unlike Brutus, neither Antony nor Octavius appears on stage in the midst of battle, and there is no single combat between the leaders. Imperial Rome can be shown in the stage fighting to be based on efficient, even faceless, military organization rather than individual valour. But other stage options are also available.

16 to the end Lucilius again emphasizes the integrity and standing of Brutus by proudly stating that Brutus will never be taken alive, but will be found 'like Brutus, like himself' (l. 25). Antony's magnanimous response (the first time we have seen him so) is likely to appear in performance to derive from his respect for Brutus, thus further elevating Brutus morally even as he appears to be approaching defeat militarily.

Act V, scene v

1–3 Following the confident exit of Antony and his soldiers comes a complete contrast in energy and mood: the exhausted entrance of Brutus and a few followers to rest. Some may be wounded; one evidently goes straight to sleep (cf. l. 32). Torches (or modern lighting effects) may signify night. Just as the Statilius reported killed after signalling with a torch is unknown, so too the 'poor remains of friends' (l. 1) with Brutus are new to the audience. Even in defeat, however, Brutus is still accompanied by loyal companions.

4–29   This section, in which Brutus (as in Plutarch; see p. 101) is refused by three of his men in turn when he asks them to assist him in suicide, develops partly in mime, with significant stage movement and strong emotion. First Brutus invites Clitus to sit down beside him; after Brutus whispers to him, the audience probably sees Clitus get to his feet and start back even before they hear the strong refusal. Clitus must move aside as Brutus calls Dardanius to him, but observes closely an identical reaction. The shocked Dardanius, in fact, moves back from Brutus far enough for Clitus to establish that Brutus has sought the same assistance from each of them in turn. From a distance they observe 'that noble vessel' (l. 13) Brutus silently weeping.

Has Volumnius observed the first two exchanges? When Brutus calls him over the audience learns that the ghost of Caesar has appeared again, and that Brutus is convinced his 'hour is come' (l. 20). To the sound of distant '*Low alarums*', Brutus effectively admits defeat, like an animal herded to the slaughter (or the grave): 'Our enemies have beat us to the pit' (l. 23). But once again a companion refuses to help Brutus die: 'That's not an office for a friend, my lord' (l. 29). He too may move away out of respect, pity, fear, awe, or a combination of complex emotions, leaving Brutus isolated on stage. Or he may be standing close as a friend when Clitus sounds the alarm.

30–44   Clitus may have taken up a position as a lookout during the previous exchange; and the renewed alarum may be louder, reinforcing Clitus' urgent 'Fly, fly' (l. 30). Brutus, however, is not to be rushed. He probably shakes hands with each soldier individually, including the newly awakened Strato, who is now identified. In his leave-taking speech Brutus puts aside defeat and despair, and like a true leader encourages his men with a cheerful aspect. This quiet moment, despite the crisis of battle nearby, gives Brutus' final words great emotional power, as in Plutarch (see pp. 100–1): he rejoices that throughout his life he 'found no man but he was true to me' (l. 35), a claim physically reinforced now as earlier by the sight of loyal followers surrounding him. He does not mention Caesar, but as he sacrificed Caesar he will nobly sacrifice himself, with no doubts at all about the greater honour of his own role compared to that of Octavius and Antony and their 'vile conquest' (l. 38). He is ready to die: 'my bones would rest' (l. 41).

This elegiac mood is broken by a loud *'Alarum'* and panic-stricken offstage shouts of *'Fly, fly, fly!'* (l. 42.1). Brutus and the soldiers will respond, but the audience will know, as may the soldiers, that when Brutus urges them on and says he will follow, he intends to take his own life. The manner of their departure – reluctantly, in panic, or against their better judgement – will again say much about Brutus.

45–52.1 Brutus holds back the last of his followers, Strato, who was asleep during the earlier threefold refusal to assist Brutus to suicide. Strato agrees, but only if he may shake Brutus' hand first. Now, finally, Brutus salutes Caesar, whose unquiet ghost will, as would be the case in *Hamlet*, rest easy after his killer's death. Brutus may run on his sword first, thus reserving the special emphasis of dying to give weight to his words; or he may speak first, before the sharp finality of the sword. Some directors have chosen to have Strato doubled by the actor who played Caesar, his face being seen only as Brutus dies, but this sort of metatheatrical actualization of Caesar stalking the battlefield carries the danger of distracting the audience from intensification around Brutus' death.

52.2 to the end As Strato stands looking down on the body of Brutus, offstage sounds again tell a story: *'Alarum. Retreat'* (l. 52.2). The drums of battle are replaced by a trumpet sounding the retreat (recognizable to an Elizabethan theatre audience as recalling troops from pursuit). Thus when Antony and Octavius enter with captives and their army, their victory is clear. As Octavius ascertains how Brutus died, and offers an amnesty to all Brutus' followers, the stage picture may throw the new emperor into prominence, or may alternatively make the dead Brutus the central focus, respectfully surrounded by friends and foes alike. Lighting and sound effects will reinforce the body language and grouping. Antony may have crossed immediately to the dead Brutus, his emotional sympathy more highly attuned than that of Octavius.

Certainly Antony's eulogy for Brutus starting 'This was the noblest Roman of them all' (l. 69) is justly famous now as a generous tribute that sums up much of what the audience has heard and seen during the play. As everyone stands quiet on the stage, Antony (following

Plutarch; see p. 95) vindicates Brutus' claim that he acted honourably –
he only, says Antony, dismissing all the rest as acting 'in envy of great
Caesar' (l. 71). The quiet, judicious words, leading to the majestic summation 'This was a man' (l. 76), tend to reinforce a sense of Brutus' tragic
stature. If we seek an approving judgement of Brutus, Antony provides
it in a solemn and moving speech.

Conventionally the senior figure on stage speaks the final words in
a Shakespearean tragedy, and Octavius here does so in conventional
language that arranges, as Fortinbras was to do in *Hamlet*, that the dead
hero should be honourably taken to burial, while the victors re-establish
order and peace. The command to 'call the field to rest' (l. 81) is a require-
ment for fresh trumpet calls, and the drums will probably play a dead
march as soldiers take up the body and exit in formal procession.

In production, however, especially when the play is done as part
of a 'Roman season', directors have sometimes chosen to amplify the
friction evident between Octavius and Antony at V.i.16–20, and to
foreshadow the war to come between them in *Antony and Cleopatra*.
Octavius may play against the text by making 'According to his virtue'
(l. 77) seem a contradiction to Antony's praise, by stressing (counter to
the metre) '*my* tent' (l. 79), and perhaps by exiting in a different direction from Antony. In such a staging, formal closure is replaced by the
beginnings of new political strife.

3   The Play's Sources and Cultural Context

When Shakespeare was composing *Julius Caesar* for its first performance in 1599 he was rapidly maturing as a playwright. With *Henry V* he
had just completed his second tetralogy of English history plays, and
Hamlet, his next tragedy, was probably already in his mind even before
he finished *Julius Caesar*. The twin golden comedies, *As You Like It* and
Twelfth Night, were also written about this time. As an artist, Shakespeare was developing his ability to explore the interior workings of
psychology, emotions, and complex personal relations.

In dramatizing the assassination of Julius Caesar and the destruction that followed, Shakespeare was choosing the most famous figure
in world history, as understood at the end of the sixteenth century.
Rome, to an Elizabethan, conjured up an image of grandeur, mag-
nificence and nobility of action and rhetoric, of a heightened sense
of stoic constancy and elevated purpose; as well as an extraordinary
predilection for bloodshed and an admiration for death by suicide. At
grammar school in Stratford the young Shakespeare would have read
Caesar, as well as what Livy, Virgil, and Cicero had to say about him.
As a playwright in London he may have read sympathetic descrip-
tions of Caesar by other classical writers such as Appian, Suetonius,
and Tacitus, as well as less favourable views by Lucan and other more
hostile writers.

The debate over Caesar had continued up to Shakespeare's own
time in histories, literature, and in the theatre. Dante confined Brutus
and Cassius to the lowest circle of hell, while Montaigne sympathized
with their Republicanism. The number of plays (nearly all now lost)
dealing with Caesar is further testimony to popular as well as learned
interest in 'the mightiest Julius' (*Hamlet* Q2, I.i.106.2).

In 1599 dramatization of Caesar's character, actions, and assassination would have been seen in a context in which Roman debate over

Republic versus Empire mirrored contemporary controversy over commonwealth versus providential rule (or divine right of kings). Queen Elizabeth's protestant England was beset by Puritans on one side, demanding greater freedom of conscience for the individual, and recognition of the role of the people and parliament (the commonwealth) in a contract of governance; and by Catholics on the other, often questioning Elizabeth's very right to rule. European Catholic hostility extended to the pope excommunicating Elizabeth in 1570, to the intended invasion and deposition of Elizabeth by the Spanish Armada in 1588, and to assassination attempts (justified by Jesuit apologists) that continued right up to and including the year Shakespeare's *Julius Caesar* appeared.

Elizabeth was nearing the end of her life, the succession was uncertain, and threats abounded. Daily church prayers for the queen, and homilies from the pulpit about subjects' absolute duty of obedience to their anointed sovereign (as of children to parents, wives to husbands, and the church to God) were political as much as religious, for the danger to Elizabeth and England was real. Debate over tyrannicide, whether in classical Rome or English history, was immediate.

In Thomas North's 1597 translation of Plutarch's *Lives of the Noble Grecians and Romans Compared*, Shakespeare found a source for his play that offered both the simple version of the story that the playwright had often made use of in earlier plays, and a much more complex mixture of high-mindedness and resultant catastrophe on both sides. He read of an autocratic but magnificent Caesar, and assassins who propelled Rome into vicious civil war and destruction; but he also read of the political illegality and destructiveness of Caesar's ambitions, and of the idealism and virtues of Brutus and the other defenders of Rome's ancient Republican freedoms. The personal and the political were interwoven in a way that suited Shakespeare's growing concern (already evident in *Henry V*, and about to be so in *Hamlet*) for the anguish of trying to reconcile political action with private morality.

In the various selections that follow, designed to give a sketch of concerns at the time Shakespeare was writing, as well as more substantial extracts from North's Plutarch that repay close attention to just how Shakespeare mined and transformed his sources, spelling and some punctuation have been modernized.

The Geneva Bible (1587 edn)

And it came to pass in those days, that there went out a decree from Caesar Augustus, that all the world should be taxed.

(Luke 2: 1)

*   *   *

Then [Jesus] saith unto them, Render therefore unto Caesar the things which are Caesar's; and unto God the things that are God's.

(Matthew 22: 21)

From *Certain Sermons or Homilies Appointed to be Read in Churches in the Time of the Late Queen Elizabeth of Famous Memory* (1635)

Almighty God hath created and appointed all things in heaven, earth, and waters, in a most excellent and perfect order. In heaven he hath appointed distinct and several orders and states of Archangels and Angels. In earth he hath assigned and appointed Kings, Princes, with other governors under them, in all good and necessary order. . . . For where there is not right order, there reigneth all abuse, carnal liberty, enormity, sin, and Babylonical confusion.

*   *   *

The wicked judge Pilate said to Christ, 'Knowest thou not I have power to crucify thee, and have power also to loose thee?' Jesus answered, 'Thou couldest have no power at all against me, except it were given thee from above.' Whereby Christ taught us plainly, that even the wicked rulers have their power, and authority from God, and therefore it is not lawful for their subjects to withstand them, although they abuse their power.

*   *   *

You have heard before in this Sermon of good order, and obedience, manifestly proved both by the Scriptures, and examples, that all subjects are bounden to obey their Magistrate, and for no cause to resist, or withstand, or rebel, or make any sedition against them, yea, although they be wicked men. . . . Therefore let us all fear the most detestable vice of rebellion, ever knowing and remembering that he that resisteth or withstandeth common authority, resisteth or withstandeth God.

From *A Conference about the Next Succession to the Crown of England* (1594) by R. Doleman [actually the Jesuit Robert Parsons], justifying the deposition of Queen Elizabeth I

The question is first, whether Richard the Second were justly deposed or no. . . . And touching the first of these three points, which is that a king upon just causes may be deposed . . . all kingly authority is given them only by the commonwealth, and that with this express condition, that they shall govern according to law and equity . . . which end being taken away or perverted, the king becometh a tyrant, a tiger, a fierce lion, a ravening wolf, a public enemy, and a bloody murderer; which were against all reason, both natural and moral, that a commonwealth could not deliver itself from so eminent a destruction.

Queen Elizabeth I, commenting on the historical (and Shakespearean) example of the deposition and assassination of a ruler

I am Richard II. Know ye not that?

From *The Book of the Governor,* by Sir Thomas Elyot (1531)

Julius Caesar, who being not able to sustain the burden of Fortune, and envying his own felicity, abandoned his natural disposition and, as it were, being drunk with overmuch wealth, sought new ways how to be advanced above the estate of mortal princes. . . . whereby he so did alienate from him the hearts of his most wise and assured adherents that, from that time forward, his life was to them tedious; and abhorring him as a monster or common enemy, they being knit in a confederacy slew him sitting in the Senate.

* * *

Julius Caesar . . . by his ambition caused to be slain . . . people innumerable, and subverted the best and most noble public weal of the world.

From the translator's dedication to Appian's *Ancient History and Exquisite Chronicle of the Roman Wars* (1578)

How God plagueth them that conspire against their Prince, this History declareth at the full. For all of them that conjured against *Caius Caesar*, not one did escape violent death. The which this Author hath a pleasure to declare, because he would affray all men from disloyalty toward their Sovereign.

From the Epilogue to *Caesar Interfectus* [*Caesar Murdered*], by Richard Eedes (performed in Latin at Oxford, 1581/2)

Caesar triumphed forcibly over the Republic; Brutus over Caesar. The former could do no more, the latter wished for nothing more; neither of them was more at fault than the other. There is something for me to praise in both; there is something in both for me to regard as vicious. It was evil that Caesar seized the Republic; good that he seized it without slaughter or bloodshed. Brutus acted rightly when he restored its liberty; but wickedly when he thought to restore it by killing Caesar. The former's moderation in victory almost veiled the vileness of his crime; the ungrateful cruelty of the latter darkened the glory of his achievement. The former behaved admirably in the worst, the latter reprehensibly in the best, of causes.

From Ovid's *Metamorphoses*, trans. Arthur Golding (1567)

The turning to a blazing star of Julius Caesar shows
That fame and immortality of virtuous doing grows.

From Plutarch's *Lives of the Noble Grecians and Romans Compared*, trans. Thomas North (1579)

From The Life of Marcus Brutus

Marcus Brutus came of that Junius Brutus for whom the ancient Romans made his statue of brass to be set up in the Capitol with the images of the kings, holding a naked sword in his hand because he had valiantly put down the Tarquins from their kingdom of Rome.

* * *

But for Brutus, his friends and countrymen, both by divers procurements, and sundry rumours of the city, and by many bills also, did openly call and procure him to do that he did. For, under the image of his ancestor Junius Brutus, that drove the kings out of Rome, they wrote: 'O, that it pleased the gods thou wert now alive, Brutus'. And again, 'That thou wert here among us now'. His tribunal, or chair, where he gave audience during the time he was Praetor, was full of such bills: 'Brutus, thou art asleep, and art not Brutus in deed'.

And of all this, Caesar's flatterers were the cause; who besides many other exceeding and unspeakable honours they daily devised for him, in the night-time they did put diadems upon the heads of his images, supposing thereby to allure the common people to call him King, instead of Dictator. Howbeit it turned to the contrary, as we have written more at large in Julius Caesar's *Life*.

Now when Cassius felt his friends, and did stir them up against Caesar, they all agreed and promised to take part with him, so Brutus were the chief of their conspiracy. For they told him that so high an enterprise and attempt as that, did not so much require men of manhood and courage to draw their swords, as it stood them upon to have a man of such estimation as Brutus, to make every man boldly think that by his only presence the fact were holy and just. If he took not this course, then that they should go to it with fainter hearts, and when they had done it they should be more fearful; because every man would think that Brutus would not have refused to have made one with them if the cause had been good and honest.

Therefore Cassius, considering this matter with himself, did first of all speak to Brutus since they grew strange together for the suit they had for the Praetorship. So when he was reconciled to him again, and that they had embraced one another, Cassius asked him if he were determined to be in the Senate house the first day of the month of March, because he heard say that Caesar's friends should move the council that day that Caesar should be called King by the Senate. Brutus answered him, he would not be there. 'But if we be sent for,' said Cassius, 'how then?' 'For myself then,' said Brutus, 'I mean not to hold my peace, but to withstand it, and rather die than lose my liberty'.

Cassius being bold, and taking hold of this word, 'Why', quoth he, 'what Roman is he alive that will suffer thee to die for the liberty? What, knowest thou not that thou art Brutus? Thinkest thou that they be cobblers, tapsters, or suchlike base mechanical people, that write these bills and scrolls which are found daily in thy Praetor's chair, and not the noblest men and best citizens that do it? No, be thou well assured, that of other Praetors they look for gifts, common distributions amongst the people, and for common plays, and to see fencers fight at the sharp, to show the people pastime. But at thy hands they specially require, as a due debt unto them, the taking away of the tyranny, being fully bent to suffer any extremity for thy sake, so that thou wilt show thyself to be the man thou art taken for, and that they hope thou art.' Thereupon he kissed Brutus, and embraced him. And so, each taking leave of other, they went both to speak with their friends about it.

Now amongst Pompey's friends there was one called Caius Ligarius, who had been accused unto Caesar for taking part with Pompey, and Caesar discharged him. But Ligarius thanked not Caesar so much for his discharge, as he was offended with him for that he was brought in danger by his tyrannical power. And therefore in his heart he was alway his mortal enemy, and was besides very familiar with Brutus, who went to see him being sick in his bed, and said unto him: 'O Ligarius, in what a time art thou sick!' Ligarius rising up in his bed, and taking him by the right hand, said unto him: 'Brutus', said he, 'if thou hast any great enterprise in hand worthy of thyself, I am whole'.

* * *

Furthermore, the only name and great calling of Brutus did bring on the most of them to give consent to this conspiracy; who having never taken oaths together, nor taken or given any caution or assurance, nor binding themselves one to another by any religious oaths, they all kept the matter so secret to themselves and could so cunningly handle it that, notwithstanding the gods did reveal it by manifest signs and tokens from above, and by predictions of sacrifices, yet all this would not be believed.

* * *

His wife Portia . . . being excellently well seen in philosophy, loving her husband well, and being of a noble courage, as she was also wise – because she would not ask her husband what he ailed before she had made some proof by her self – she took a little razor such as barbers occupy to pare men's nails, and, causing her maids and women to go out of her chamber, gave herself a great gash withal in her thigh, that she was straight all of a gore blood; and, incontinently after, a vehement fever took her, by reason of the pain of her wound.

Then perceiving her husband was marvellously out of quiet and that he could take no rest, even in her greatest pain of all she spake in this sort unto him: 'I being, O Brutus', said she, 'the daughter of Cato, was married unto thee not to be thy bedfellow and companion in bed and at board only, like a harlot; but to be partaker also with thee of thy good and evil fortune. Now for thyself, I can find no cause of fault in thee touching our match, but for my part, how may I show my duty towards thee, and how much I would do for thy sake, if I cannot constantly bear a secret mischance or grief with thee, which requireth secrecy and fidelity? I confess that a woman's wit commonly is too weak to keep a secret safely. But yet, Brutus, good education and the company of virtuous men have some power to reform the defect of nature. And for myself, I have this benefit moreover: that I am the daughter of Cato, and wife of Brutus. This notwithstanding, I did not trust to any of these things before, until that now I have found by experience that no pain nor grief whatsoever can overcome me.'

With those words she showed him her wound on her thigh, and told him what she had done to prove herself. Brutus was amazed to hear what she said unto him, and lifting up his hands to heaven he besought the gods to give him the grace he might bring his enterprise to so good pass, that he might be found a husband worthy of so noble a wife as Portia. So he then did comfort her the best he could.

*   *   *

... it was one of the porches about the Theatre, in the which there was a certain place full of seats for men to sit in, where also was set up the image of Pompey, which the city had made and consecrated in honour of him, when he did beautify that part of the city with the Theatre he built, with divers porches about it. In this place was the assembly of the Senate appointed to be, just on the fifteenth day of the month of March, which the Romans call *Idus Martias*. So that it seemed some god of purpose had brought Caesar thither to be slain, for revenge of Pompey's death.

*   *   *

Portia being very careful and pensive for that which was to come, and being too weak to away with so great and inward grief of mind, she could hardly keep within, but was frighted with every little noise and cry she heard, as those that are taken and possessed with the fury of the Bacchantes, asking every man that came from the marketplace what Brutus did, and still sent messenger after messenger, to know what news. At length, Caesar's coming being prolonged as you have heard, Portia's weakness was not able to hold out any longer, and thereupon she suddenly swooned, that she had no leisure to go to her chamber, but was taken in the midst of her house, where her speech and senses failed her.

* * *

Popilius Laena, that had talked before with Brutus and Cassius and had prayed the gods they might bring this enterprise to pass, went unto Caesar and kept him a long time with a talk. Caesar gave good ear unto him. Wherefore the conspirators (if so they should be called), not hearing what he said to Caesar, but conjecturing, by that he had told them a little before, that his talk was none other but the very discovery of their conspiracy, they were afraid every man of them, and, one looking in another's face, it was easy to see that they all were of a mind, that it was no tarrying for them till they were apprehended, but rather that they should kill themselves with their own hands. And when Cassius and certain other clapped their hands on their swords under their gowns to draw them, Brutus, marking the countenance and gesture of Laena, and considering that he did use himself rather like an humble and earnest suitor than like an accuser, he said nothing to his companion (because there were many amongst them that were not of the conspiracy), but with a pleasant countenance encouraged Cassius. And immediately after, Laena went from Caesar and kissed his hand; which showed plainly that it was for some matter concerning himself that he had held him so long in talk.

* * *

But Brutus and his consorts, having their swords bloody in their hands, went straight to the Capitol, persuading the Romans, as they went, to take their liberty again. Now at the first time, when the murder was newly done, there were sudden outcries of people that ran up and down the city, the which indeed did the more increase the fear and tumult. But when they saw they slew no man, neither did spoil or make havoc of anything, then certain of the Senators, and many of the people, emboldening themselves, went to the Capitol unto them. There a great number of men being assembled together one after another, Brutus made an oration unto them to win the favour of the people, and to justify that they had done. All those that were by said they had done well, and cried unto them that they should boldly come down from the Capitol. Whereupon, Brutus and his companions came boldly down into the marketplace. The rest followed in troop; but Brutus went foremost, very honourably compassed in round about with the noblest men of the city, which brought him from the Capitol, through the marketplace, to the pulpit for orations. When the people saw him in the pulpit, although they were a multitude of rakehells of all sorts and had a good will to make some stir, yet, being ashamed to do it for the reverence they bare unto Brutus, they kept silence, to hear what he would say. When Brutus began to speak, they gave him quiet audience.

*　*　*

The Senate being called again to council . . . came to talk of Caesar's will and testament, and of his funerals and tomb. Then Antonius thinking good his testament should be read openly, and also that his body should be honourably buried, and not in hugger-mugger, lest the people might thereby take occasion to be worse offended if they did otherwise, Cassius stoutly spoke against it. But Brutus went with the motion, and agreed unto it. Wherein it seemeth he committed a second fault. For the first fault he did was when he would not consent to his fellow conspirators that Antonius should be slain; and therefore he was justly accused, that thereby he had saved and strengthened a strong and grievous enemy of their conspiracy. The second fault was when he agreed that Caesar's funerals should be as Antonius would have them; the which indeed marred all. For first of all, when Caesar's testament was openly read among them, whereby it appeared that he bequeathed unto every citizen of Rome seventy-five drachmas a man, and that he left his gardens and arbours unto the people, which he had on this side of the river of Tiber, in the place where now the Temple of Fortune is built, the people then loved him, and were marvellous sorry for him.

*　*　*

But there was a poet called Cinna, who had been no partaker of the conspiracy, but was alway one of Caesar's chiefest friends. He dreamed, the night before, that Caesar bade him to supper with him, and that he refusing to go, Caesar was very importunate with him, and compelled him; so that at length he led him by the hand into a great dark place, where, being marvellously afraid, he was driven to follow him in spite of his heart. This dream put him all night into a fever. And yet, notwithstanding, the next morning when he heard that they carried Caesar's body to burial, being ashamed not to accompany his funerals, he went out of his house, and thrust himself into the press of the common people that were in a great uproar. And because some one called him by his name, Cinna, the people, thinking he had been that Cinna who in an oration he made had spoken very evil of Caesar, they, falling upon him in their rage slew him outright in the marketplace.

*   *   *

For it was said that Antonius spake it openly divers times, that he thought that of all them that had slain Caesar, there was none but Brutus only that was moved to do it as thinking the act commendable of itself; but that all the other conspirators did conspire his death for some private malice or envy that they otherwise did bear unto him.

*   *   *

Therefore, before they fell in hand with any other matter, [Brutus and Cassius] went into a little chamber together, and bade every man avoid, and did shut the doors to them. Then they began to pour out their complaints one to the other, and grew hot and loud, earnestly accusing one another, and at length fell both a-weeping. Their friends that were without the chamber hearing them loud within and angry between themselves, they were both amazed, and afraid also lest it would grow to further matter. But yet they were commanded that no man should come to them. . . . Brutus, upon complaint of the Sardians, did condemn and noted Lucius Pella for a defamed person, that had been a Praetor of the Romans and whom Brutus had given charge unto; for that he was accused and convicted of robbery and pilfery in his office. This judgement much misliked Cassius. . . . And therefore he greatly reproved Brutus for that he would show himself so strait and severe, in such a time as was meeter to bear a little, than to take things at the worst. Brutus in contrary manner answered that he should remember the Ides of March, at which time they slew Julius Caesar.

*   *   *

Brutus was a careful man and slept very little, both for that his diet was moderate, as also because he was continually occupied. He never slept in the daytime, and in the night no longer than the time he was driven to be alone, and when everybody else took their rest. But now whilst he was in war, and his head ever busily occupied to think of his affairs, and what would happen, after he had slumbered a little after supper, he spent all the rest of the night in dispatching of his weightiest causes; and after he had taken order for them, if he had any leisure left him, he would read some book till the third watch of the night, at what time the captains, petty-captains, and colonels did use to come unto him.

So, being ready to go into Europe, one night very late, when all the camp took quiet rest, as he was in his tent with a little light, thinking of weighty matters, he thought he heard one come in to him, and casting his eye towards the door of his tent, that he saw a wonderful strange and monstrous shape of a body coming towards him, and said never a word. So Brutus boldly asked what he was, a god, or a man, and what cause brought him thither. The spirit answered him: 'I am thy evil spirit, Brutus; and thou shalt see me by the city of Philippes'. Brutus, being no otherwise afraid, replied again unto it: 'Well, then I shall see thee again'. The spirit presently vanished away; and Brutus called his men unto him, who told him that they heard no noise, nor saw anything at all.

* * *

Cassius was of opinion not to try this war at one battle, but rather to delay time, and to draw it out in length, considering that they were the stronger in money, and the weaker in men and armours. But Brutus, in contrary manner, did alway before, and at that time also, desire nothing more than to put all to the hazard of battle as soon as might be possible, to the end he might either quickly restore his country to her former liberty, or rid him forthwith of this miserable world. . . .

Cassius . . . took [Messala] by the hand, and holding him fast, in token of kindness as his manner was, told him in Greek: 'Messala, I protest unto thee, and make thee my witness, that I am compelled against my mind and will (as Pompey the Great was) to jeopard the liberty of our country to the hazard of a battle. And yet we must be lively and of good courage, considering our good fortune, whom we should wrong too much to mistrust her, although we follow evil counsel.' Messala writeth that Cassius having spoken these last words unto him, he bade him farewell, and willed him to come to supper to him the next night following, because it was his birthday.

The next morning, by break of day, the signal of battle was set out in Brutus' and Cassius' camp, which was an arming scarlet coat; and both the chieftains spoke together in the midst of their armies. There Cassius began to speak first, and said: 'The gods grant us, O Brutus, that this day we may win the field, and ever after to live all the rest of our life quietly, one with another. But sith the gods have so ordained it that the greatest and chiefest things amongst men are most uncertain, and that, if the battle fall out otherwise today than we wish or look for, we shall hardly meet again, what art thou then determined to do: to fly, or die?'

Brutus answered him: 'Being yet but a young man and not over greatly experienced in the world, I trust (I know not how) a certain rule of philosophy by the which I did greatly blame and reprove Cato for killing of himself, as being no lawful nor godly act, touching the gods, nor, concerning men, valiant; not to give place and yield to divine providence, and not constantly and patiently to take whatsoever it pleaseth him to send us, but to draw back and fly. But being now in the midst of the danger, I am of a contrary mind. For, if it be not the will of God that this battle fall out fortunate for us, I will look no more for hope, neither seek to make any new supply for war again, but will rid me of this miserable world, and content me with my fortune. For I gave up my life for my country in the Ides of March, for the which I shall live in another more glorious world.' Cassius fell a-laughing to hear what he said, and embracing him: 'Come on then', said he, 'let us go and charge our enemies with this mind. For either we shall conquer, or we shall not need to fear the conquerors.'

After this talk, they fell to consultation among their friends for the ordering of the battle. Then Brutus prayed Cassius he might have the leading of the right wing, the which men thought was far meeter for Cassius, both because he was the elder man, and also for that he had the better experience. But yet Cassius gave it him, and willed that Messala, who had charge of one of the warlikest legions they had, should be also in that wing with Brutus.

* * *

Furthermore, the vaward, and the midst of Brutus' battle, had already put all their enemies to flight that withstood them, with great slaughter; so that Brutus had conquered all on his side, and Cassius had lost all on the other side. For nothing undid them but that Brutus went not to help Cassius, thinking he had overcome them, as himself had done; and Cassius on the other side tarried not for Brutus, thinking he had been overthrown, as himself was. . . .

But with tarrying too long also, more than through the valiantness or foresight of the captains his enemies, Cassius found himself compassed in with the right wing of his enemies' army. Whereupon his horsemen broke immediately, and fled for life towards the sea. Furthermore, perceiving his footmen to give ground, he did what he could to keep them from flying, and took an ensign from one of the ensign-bearers that fled, and stuck it fast at his feet; although with much ado he could scant keep his own guard together.

So Cassius himself was at length compelled to fly, with a few about him, unto a little hill from whence they might easily see what was done in all the plain; howbeit Cassius himself saw nothing, for his sight was very bad, saving that he saw, and yet with much ado, how the enemies spoiled his camp before his eyes. He saw also a great troop of horsemen whom Brutus sent to aid him, and thought that they were his enemies that followed him. But yet he sent Titinnius, one of them that was with him, to go and know what they were. Brutus' horsemen saw him coming afar off, whom when they knew that he was one of Cassius' chiefest friends, they shouted out for joy; and they that were familiarly acquainted with him lighted from their horses, and went and embraced him. The rest compassed him in round about a-horseback, with songs of victory and great rushing of their harness, so that they made all the field ring again for joy.

But this marred all. For Cassius thinking indeed that Titinnius was taken of the enemies, he then spake these words: 'Desiring too much to live, I have lived to see one of my best friends taken, for my sake, before my face'. After that, he got into a tent where nobody was, and took Pindarus with him, one of his freed bondmen, whom he reserved ever for such a pinch, since the cursed battle of the Parthians where Crassus was slain, though he notwithstanding scaped from that overthrow. But then casting his cloak over his head, and holding out his bare neck unto Pindarus, he gave him his head to be stricken off. So the head was found severed from the body. But after that time Pindarus was never seen more. . . .

By and by they knew the horsemen that came towards them, and might see Titinnius crowned with a garland of triumph, who came before with great speed unto Cassius. But when he perceived, by the cries and tears of his friends which tormented themselves, the misfortune that had chanced to his captain Cassius by mistaking, he drew out his sword, cursing himself a thousand times that he had tarried so long, and so slew himself presently in the field. Brutus in the meantime came forward still, and understood also that Cassius had been overthrown. But he knew nothing of his death, till he came very near to his camp. So when he was come thither, after he had lamented the death of Cassius, calling him the last of all the Romans, being unpossible that Rome should ever breed again so noble and valiant a man as he, he caused his body to be buried.

* * *

But that which won him the victory at the first battle, did now lose it him at the second. For at the first time, the enemies that were broken and fled were straight cut in pieces; but at the second battle, of Cassius' men that were put to flight, there were few slain; and they that saved themselves by speed, being afraid because they had been overcome, did discourage the rest of the army when they came to join with them, and filled all the army with fear and disorder.

There was the son of M. Cato slain, valiantly fighting amongst the lusty youths. For, notwithstanding that he was very weary, and overharried, yet would he not therefore fly, but manfully fighting and laying about him, telling aloud his name and also his father's name, at length he was beaten down amongst many other dead bodies of his enemies, which he had slain, round about him. So there were slain in the field all the chiefest gentlemen and nobility that were in his army, who valiantly ran into any danger to save Brutus' life.

Amongst them there was one of Brutus' friends called Lucilius, who seeing a troop of barbarous men making no reckoning of all men else they met in their way, but going all together right against Brutus, he determined to stay them with the hazard of his life, and being left behind, told them that he was Brutus; and, because they should believe him, he prayed them to bring him to Antonius, for he said he was afraid of Caesar, and that he did trust Antonius better.

These barbarous men being very glad of this good hap, and thinking themselves happy men, they carried him in the night, and sent some before unto Antonius to tell him of their coming. He was marvellous glad of it, and went out to meet them that brought him. Others also understanding of it, that they had brought Brutus prisoner, they came out of all parts of the camp to see him, some pitying his hard fortune, and others saying that it was not done like himself, so cowardly to be taken alive of the barbarous people for fear of death. When they came near together, Antonius stayed awhile, bethinking himself how he should use Brutus.

In the meantime Lucilius was brought to him, who stoutly with a bold countenance said: 'Antonius, I dare assure thee that no enemy hath taken nor shall take Marcus Brutus alive; and I beseech God keep him from that fortune. For wheresoever he be found, alive or dead, he will be found like himself. And now for myself, I am come unto thee, having deceived these men of arms here, bearing them down that I was Brutus; and do not refuse to suffer any torment thou wilt put me to.'

Lucilius' words made them all amazed that heard him. Antonius on the other side, looking upon all them that had brought him, said unto them: 'My companions, I think ye are sorry you have failed of your purpose, and that you think this man hath done you great wrong. But, I do assure you, you have taken a better booty than that you followed. For, instead of an enemy, you have brought me a friend; and for my part, if you had brought me Brutus alive, truly I cannot tell what I should have done to him. For I had rather have such men my friends, as this man here, than enemies.' Then he embraced Lucilius, and at that time delivered him to one of his friends in custody; and Lucilius ever after served him faithfully, even to his death.

* * *

Now, the night being far spent, Brutus as he sat bowed towards Clitus, one of his men and told him somewhat in his ear; the other answered him not, but fell a-weeping. Thereupon he proved Dardanus, and said somewhat also to him. At length he came to Volumnius himself, and speaking to him in Greek, prayed him, for the study's sake which brought them acquainted together, that he would help him to put his hand to his sword, to thrust it in him to kill him. Volumnius denied his request, and so did many others; and, amongst the rest, one of them said, there was no tarrying for them there, but that they must needs fly. . . .

Then, taking every man by the hand, he said these words unto them with a cheerful countenance: 'It rejoiceth my heart that not one of my friends hath failed me at my need, and I do not complain of my fortune, but only for my country's sake. For, as for me, I think myself happier than they that have overcome, considering that I leave a perpetual fame of our courage and manhood, the which our enemies the conquerors

shall never attain unto by force nor money, neither can let their pos-
terity to say, that they being naughty and unjust men, have slain good
men, to usurp tyrannical power not pertaining to them.'

Having said so... he went a little aside with two or three only, among
the which Strato was one.... Strato, at his request, held the sword in his
hand, and turned his head aside, and that Brutus fell down upon it; and
so ran himself through, and died presently.

Messala . . . brought Strato, Brutus' friend, unto [Octavius] and
weeping said: 'Caesar, behold, here is he that did the last service to my
Brutus.'

From *The Life of Julius Caesar*

This was the last war that Caesar made. But the Triumph he made into
Rome for the same did as much offend the Romans, and more, than
anything that ever he had done before; because he had not overcome
captains that were strangers, nor barbarous kings, but had destroyed
the sons of the noblest man in Rome, whom fortune had overthrown.
And because he had plucked up his race by the roots, men did not think
it meet for him to triumph so for the calamities of his country....

And now for himself, after he had ended his civil wars, he did
so honourably behave himself, that there was no fault to be found
in him.... For he pardoned many of them that had borne arms against
him, and furthermore, did prefer some of them to honour and office
in the commonwealth: as, amongst others, Cassius and Brutus, both
the which were made Praetors. And where Pompey's images had been
thrown down, he caused them to be set up again; whereupon Cicero
said then, that Caesar setting up Pompey's images again, he made his
own to stand the surer. And when some of his friends did counsel him
to have a guard for the safety of his person, and some also did offer
themselves to serve him, he would never consent to it, but said, it was
better to die once than always to be afraid of death.

* * *

At that time the feast Lupercalia was celebrated.... Antonius, who was
Consul at that time, was one of them that ran this holy course. So when
he came into the marketplace, the people made a lane for him to run at
liberty, and he came to Caesar and presented him a diadem wreathed
about with laurel. Whereupon there rose a certain cry of rejoicing, not

very great, done only by a few appointed for the purpose. But when
Caesar refused the diadem, then all the people together made an outcry
of joy. Then Antonius offering it him again, there was a second shout of
joy, but yet of a few. But when Caesar refused it again the second time,
then all the whole people shouted.

After that, there were set up images of Caesar in the city with diadems upon their heads, like kings. Those the two Tribunes, Flavius and
Marullus, went and pulled down. . . . Caesar was so offended withal,
that he deprived Marullus and Flavius of their Tribuneships.

*   *   *

Certainly destiny may be easier foreseen than avoided, considering the strange and wonderful signs that were said to be seen before
Caesar's death. For, touching the fires in the element, and spirits running up and down in the night, and also the solitary birds to be seen
at noondays sitting in the great market-place – are not all these signs
perhaps worth the noting, in such a wonderful chance as happened?
But Strabo the Philosopher writeth that divers men were seen going
up and down in fire; and furthermore, that there was a slave of the
soldiers that did cast a marvellous burning flame out of his hand, inso-
much as they that saw it thought he had been burnt; but when the fire
was out, it was found he had no hurt. Caesar self also, doing sacrifice
unto the gods, found that one of the beasts which was sacrificed had
no heart; and that was a strange thing in nature, how a beast could live
without a heart.

Furthermore, there was a certain soothsayer that had given Caesar
warning long time afore, to take heed of the day of the ides of March
(which is the fifteenth of the month), for on that day he should be in
great danger. That day being come, Caesar going unto the Senate house
and speaking merrily unto the soothsayer, told him: 'The Ides of March
be come'. 'So be they', softly answered the soothsayer, 'but yet they are
not past'.

*   *   *

Decius Brutus . . . fearing that if Caesar did adjourn the session that
day the conspiracy would out, laughed the soothsayers to scorn; and
reproved Caesar, saying that he gave the Senate occasion to mislike
with him, and that they might think he mocked them, considering that
by his commandment they were assembled, and that they were ready
willingly to grant him all things, and to proclaim him king of all the

provinces of the Empire of Rome out of Italy, and that he should wear his diadem in all other places both by sea and land. And furthermore, that if any man should tell them, from him, they should depart for that present time, and return again when Calpurnia should have better dreams – what would his enemies and ill-wishers say?

* * *

It is also reported that Cassius (though otherwise he did favour the doctrine of Epicurus) beholding the image of Pompey before they entered into the action of their traitorous enterprise, he did softly call upon it to aid him. But the instant danger of the present time, taking away his former reason, did suddenly put him into a furious passion and made him like a man half besides himself. . . .

So, Caesar coming into the house, all the Senate stood up on their feet to do him honour. Then part of Brutus' company and confederates stood round about Caesar's chair, and part of them also came towards him, as though they made suit with Metellus Cimber, to call home his brother again from banishment. And thus, prosecuting still their suit, they followed Caesar till he was set in his chair; who denying their petitions, and being offended with them one after another, because the more they were denied, the more they pressed upon him and were the earnester with him. . . . Then Casca behind him struck him in the neck with his sword; howbeit the wound was not great nor mortal, because, it seemed, the fear of such a devilish attempt did amaze him, and take his strength from him, that he killed him not at the first blow. But, Caesar, turning straight unto him, caught hold of his sword and held it hard. And they both cried out, Caesar in Latin: 'O vile traitor Casca, what doest thou?' And Casca in Greek to his brother: 'Brother, help me.'

At the beginning of this stir, they that were present, not knowing of the conspiracy, were so amazed with the horrible sight they saw, they had no power to fly, neither to help him, not so much as once to make any outcry. They on the other side that had conspired his death compassed him in on every side with their swords drawn in their hands, that Caesar turned him nowhere but he was stricken at by some, and still had naked swords in his face, and was hacked and mangled among them, as a wild beast taken of hunters. For it was agreed among them that every man should give him a wound, because all their parts should be in this murder. And then Brutus himself gave him one wound about his privities.

Men report also that Caesar did still defend himself against the rest, running every way with his body. But when he saw Brutus with his sword drawn in his hand, then he pulled his gown over his head, and made no more resistance, and was driven, either casually or purposedly by the counsel of the conspirators, against the base whereupon Pompey's image stood, which ran all of a gore blood till he was slain.

Thus it seemed that the image took just revenge of Pompey's enemy, being thrown down on the ground at his feet, and yielding up his ghost there for the number of wounds he had upon him. For it is reported that he had three-and-twenty wounds upon his body; and divers of the conspirators did hurt themselves, striking one body with so many blows.

When Caesar was slain, the Senate, though Brutus stood in the midst amongst them as though he would have said somewhat touching this fact, presently ran out of the house, and flying filled all the city with marvellous fear and tumult.

* * *

Again, of signs in the element, the great comet which seven nights together was seen very bright after Caesar's death, the eighth night after was never seen more.

From *The Life of Marcus Antonius*

And therefore when Caesar's body was brought to the place where it should be buried, he made a funeral oration in commendation of Caesar, according to the ancient custom of praising noble men at their funerals. When he saw that the people were very glad and desirous also to hear Caesar spoken of, and his praises uttered, he mingled his oration with lamentable words, and by amplifying of matters did greatly move their hearts and affections unto pity and compassion. In fine, to conclude his oration, he unfolded before the whole assembly the bloody garments of the dead, thrust through in many places with their swords, and called the malefactors cruel and cursed murderers. With these words he put the people into such a fury, that they presently took Caesar's body, and burnt it in the marketplace with such tables and forms as they could get together. Then, when the fire was kindled, they took firebrands, and ran to the murderers' houses to set them afire and to make them come out to fight. Brutus therefore and his accomplices, for safety of their persons, were driven to fly the city.

* * *

So Octavius Caesar would not lean to Cicero, when he saw that his whole travail and endeavour was only to restore the commonwealth to her former liberty. Therefore he sent certain of his friends to Antonius, to make them friends again. And thereupon all three met together (to wit, Caesar, Antonius, and Lepidus) in an island environed round about with a little river, and there remained three days together. Now, as touching all other matters, they were easily agreed and did divide all the Empire of Rome between them, as if it had been their own inheritance.

But yet they could hardly agree whom they would put to death; for every one of them would kill their enemies, and save their kinsmen and friends. Yet at length, giving place to their greedy desire to be revenged of their enemies, they spurned all reverence of blood and holiness of friendship at their feet. For Caesar left Cicero to Antonius' will; Antonius also forsook Lucius Caesar, who was his uncle by his mother; and both of them together suffered Lepidus to kill his own brother Paulus. Yet some writers affirm that Caesar and Antonius requested Paulus might be slain, and that Lepidus was contented with it.

In my opinion there was never a more horrible, unnatural, and crueller change than this was. For, thus changing murder for murder, they did as well kill those whom they did forsake and leave unto others, as those also which others left unto them to kill; but so much more was their wickedness and cruelty great unto their friends, for that they put them to death being innocents, and having no cause to hate them.

Shakespeare on Caesar

KING HENRY   No Harry, Harry – 'tis no land of thine.
    Thy place is filled, thy sceptre wrung from thee,
    Thy balm washed off wherewith thou wast anointed.
    No bending knee will call thee Caesar now.
                (*Richard Duke of York* [*3 Henry VI*] III.i.15–18)

KING EDWARD   *Et tu, Brute* – wilt thou stab Caesar too?
                (*Richard Duke of York* [*3 Henry VI*] V.i.81)

QUEEN MARGARET   O traitors, murderers!
    They that stabbed Caesar shed no blood at all,
    Did not offend, nor were not worthy blame,
    If this foul deed were by to equal it.

                (*Richard Duke of York* [*3 Henry VI*] V.v.51–4)

LORD BARDOLPH   O, such a day,
    So fought, so followed, and so fairly won,
    Came not till now to dignify the times
    Since Caesar's fortunes.

                         (*2 Henry IV* I.i.20–3)

CHORUS   But now behold,
    In the quick forge and working-house of thought,
    How London doth pour out her citizens.
    The Mayor and all his brethren, in best sort,
    Like to the senators of th'antique Rome
    With the plebeians swarming at their heels,
    Go forth and fetch their conqu'ring Caesar in—

                      (*Henry V* Chorus 5.22–8)

HORATIO   In the most high and palmy state of Rome,
    A little ere the mightiest Julius fell,
    The graves stood tenantless, and the sheeted dead
    Did squeak and gibber in the Roman streets
    At stars with trains of fire, and dews of blood,
    Disasters in the sun; and the moist star,
    Upon whose influence Neptune's empire stands,
    Was sick almost to doomsday with eclipse.

                    (*Hamlet* Q2, I.i.106.1–.13)

POLONIUS   I did enact Julius Caesar. I was killed i'th' Capitol. Brutus
killed me.

                        (*Hamlet* III.ii.93–4)

HAMLET   Imperial Caesar, dead and turned to clay,
    Might stop a hole to keep the wind away.
    O, that that earth which kept the world in awe
    Should patch a wall t'expel the winter's flaw!

                         (*Hamlet* V.i.196–9)

LUCIO   What, at the wheels of Caesar? Art thou led in triumph?
                                        (*Measure for Measure* III.i.298–9)

IAGO   He's a soldier fit to stand by Caesar
     And give direction.
                                        (*Othello* II.iii.106–7)

FIRST LORD DUMAINE   It was a disaster of war that Caesar himself
     could not have prevented, if he had been there to command.
                                        (*All's Well That Ends Well* III.vi.47–7)

4 Key Productions and Performances

Edwin Booth and the nineteenth century

When Edwin Booth opened his famous long run in New York on Christmas Day, 1871, both he and the play were well known and popular. *Julius Caesar* had been a staple of the American stage since the American Revolution, its content well suited to republican sympathies. And Edwin Booth was the most famous actor of a notable theatrical family. 'The three sons of the great Booth' gathered to perform *Julius Caesar* as a fundraiser in 1864 ('the great Booth', by then dead, was their barn-storming father Junius Brutus Booth, named after the founder of the Roman Republic; see I.ii.158–61): Edwin played Brutus, Junius Brutus Jr. played Cassius, and Antony was played by John Wilkes. Ironically, John Wilkes Booth would only a few months later carry out the real-life assassination of President Abraham Lincoln.

Edwin Booth understandably avoided the play for a number of years after this event, but eventually mounted the 1871–72 production that held the stage, with various changes in cast, for twenty years, and may be regarded as a pre-eminent example of nineteenth-century interpretation, both in its continuation of tradition and in its significant innovation.

The nineteenth-century tradition: Kemble

We need to go back to John Philip Kemble's 1812 production at the Theatre Royal, Covent Garden in London if we are to understand Booth's importance. Kemble and his sister, Sarah Siddons, revolutionized Shakespearean staging and acting, and their influence continued to be felt throughout the rest of the century. In terms of *Julius Caesar* we might identify three aspects: the unifying and simplifying of the script, the acting of Brutus, and the introduction of spectacular sets as well as supernumeraries as 'living scenery'.

Kemble's version of the script became the standard form of the play as acted throughout the century. As with all aspects of his production, Kemble wished to improve Shakespeare's play by smoothing it and making it more unified. To this end he reduced the number of characters, and replaced most of the new ones from Acts IV and V with existing characters from earlier in the play (see pp. 2–3, 145–6). Artemidorus and the Soothsayer were conflated, and many scenes were reduced or (in the case of Cinna the Poet's III.iii, and Antony's IV.i proscription scene) eliminated. Above all, the text was trimmed to offer a grand, high-minded, and utterly consistent Brutus. Kemble 'considered the play Brutus's tragedy, with Brutus seen as the self-possessed Stoic, a magnanimous philosopher and patriot . . . not the intensely human, and often inconsistent, character created by Shakespeare' (Ripley, p. 53). The end of the play was cut so that it ended with Antony's eulogy to Brutus, 'This was the noblest Roman of them all . . . "This was a man!"' (V.v.69–76).

Kemble's second innovation was spectacle. Not only did he introduce sumptuous historically based set painting of the visual glory of Rome (Imperial Rome, however, since it was so much more spectacular than the late Republic), but costumes to match. Although Caesar himself continued to be played by a supporting actor, he was for the first time given a costume to match his rank. And he was given dozens of supporters: soldiers, standard bearers, lictors, priests, virgins, admiring citizens. Here was a visual recreation of historical Rome, and a Caesar with the full panoply of rank, visual evidence of the established power that Brutus would have to challenge.

Finally, Kemble's stately acting suited the portrayal of a classical hero. Following a tradition from at least the late seventeenth century, Kemble as the star actor played Brutus. The simplified script was the platform for his grand style of acting, which aimed to depict an ideal rather than messy and inconsistent reality. This was an abstract study of a Roman patriot, an impressive Stoic who subordinated personal emotion in favour of an elevated sense of duty to his country: 'This was the man!'

Booth's 1871 production

Booth largely followed Kemble's simplified script, and even added to its emphasis on Brutus by, for instance, delaying the entrance of Brutus and Cassius until the departure of Caesar's procession at I.ii.24. This was still the idealized and heroic Brutus who, for instance, needs no assistance to commit suicide at the end of the play. However, Booth added both human warmth and complexity to the character. One small change to the script illustrates this very well: Brutus' brief and sympathetic musing over the sleeping Lucius (II.i.230–4), cut from Kemble's version as, presumably, distractingly domestic for a classical hero, was reinstated by Booth to humanize the moral paragon.

Booth also continued but softened the Kemble tradition of spectacle. Surviving illustrations of set designs reveal a sense of architectural grandeur (again using Imperial rather than Republican Rome), but with the classical austerity modified by colour and spatial arrangements. The temples and public buildings painted for I.i and I.ii, for instance, displayed glowing sandstone, red marble pillars, and friezes of blues, greens, and reds. The costumes of the supernumeraries (including for the first time women and children) included lictors in 'scarlet Roman costume, trimmed with orange' (promptbook notation) and carrying fasces, and of course soldiers and standard bearers in scarlet and gold uniform.

The extras initially numbered about eighty in these two scenes, but the spectacle was so popular that Booth soon increased the number to over two hundred. The promptbook includes a note that for Act III '50 supers change to senators'. In the days before movies, this was indeed history come to life. But Booth did not rely simply on grandeur. The Orchard scene (II.i), for instance, used the sophisticated controllable lighting that was now available to dim the scene to an eerie gloom, illuminated occasionally by the lightning that continued from I.iii. A critic later recalled the 'poetical' image of 'that shadowy garden and the sinister forms of the conspirators when all the action was suddenly arrested by the admonition, "Peace! count the clock", and far away the bell struck three'. The promptbook instructs 'count 8 or 10 between strokes'; for a tableau to hold so long implies that an extraordinary mood must have been created for the audience. Similar lighting effects apparently made the apparition of Caesar's Ghost in IV.ii equivalently striking.

Such manipulation of mood and stage picture was part of Booth's brilliance in using the resources of nineteenth-century theatre to tell the story as he wished to. Since the play in this version is above all Brutus' story, the Assassination scene (III.i) was the focal point of the play. Booth adapted his design from a famous painting of the death of Caesar by the Romantic artist Gérôme, with a curving set of seats for the '50 supers' who had become senators. The curve (avoiding Kemble's rigid classical symmetry) allowed him to place Caesar to one side on a raised chair, beneath a statue of Pompey, and to choreograph the assassination in such a way as to throw the focus onto Brutus. As the conspirators all kneel about Caesar, Casca's first stab is their cue to rush at Caesar. Cassius then 'pulls Caesar from throne, stabs & throws him over to Brutus, who then stabs him' (promptbook). Cassius has thus ensured that Brutus will take part, but as Cassius triumphantly bestrides the dead Caesar, Brutus drops his sword, 'averts his face, raises hands in sorrow', and crosses to the opposite side of the stage where the senators are. The stage picture, in addition to being a tableau of liberty over the dead Caesar, emphasizes the reaction of Brutus. Far from triumphalist, he is already grief-stricken at what he has had to do. And while some part of the action has been relatively realistic, it is also clear how carefully the choreography and the frozen tableau that follows were planned in order to achieve a pictorial meaning.

This seems to have been the first production in which Brutus and Cassius were sharply differentiated in motive and action during the assassination. Here Booth's stagecraft and acting style are seen reinforcing each other, for Booth, although idealizing Brutus as Kemble had, did so in a different manner, romanticizing and sentimentalizing his hero where Kemble had made him austere and classical. Booth was of slight build, which for many critics made him unsuitable for a part traditionally played by actors of heroic proportions and dignity. He therefore avoided the statuesque, and instead played for a gentle melancholy and emotional complexity. The trouble of his mind suggested Hamlet. Whereas Kemble was always the Stoic, Booth, when calling for the conspirators to sacrifice Caesar, not butcher him (II.i.167–75; and see pp. 1–2), was 'aroused from his sombre, stoical mood, and kindled into deepest earnestness'; he was 'the great soul which, despite affection, could slay Caesar to save Rome'. But Booth was sufficiently Stoic that, like Kemble, his suicide at the end needed no assistance from anyone.

Cassius, by contrast (played by Lawrence Barrett), was 'choleric' and 'hot-headed', full of nervous energy, a 'fiery spirit . . . in its . . . scorn of human weakness, and its passionate hatred of tyranny'. Where Brutus was grave and still, Cassius was restless and always in movement. The Quarrel scene (IV.ii) was well served by this contrast, with Brutus standing calm 'like a great rock against the buffetings of the angry sea'.

And just as Brutus was idealized, Cassius too was portrayed in a positive manner throughout. Even as he strode over the dead Caesar in III. i, an act that would appear callous in other productions, it was clear to a contemporary critic that this Cassius was motivated by 'the sincerity of political fanaticism', not by envy or personal hatred.

In fact, when Booth himself later swapped to the role of Cassius in this production, critics compared his portrayal to the way he played Iago in *Othello*. He was 'violent, vindictive, as if inspired more by loathing of the tyrant than by hatred of tyranny'. Unlike Barrett, Booth's 'eye expresses, instead of frankness, exultation at the prospect of success'. Thus a change of actors, even within the same production, could result in a significantly different play.

Booth also, before the run ended, briefly took on the role of Mark Antony, thus becoming the first actor ever to have played Brutus, Cassius, and Antony all in the same production. Antony was at this time regarded as a supporting role, with the rhetorical skill of the Forum speech the main demand on the actor. However, Booth emphasized Antony first as an urbane courtier to Caesar, and then, in violent contrast, displaying a 'concentrated intensity of hate, animosity and vengeful fire'. The acting potential of Antony was to be much further extended before the century ended.

Beerbohm Tree's 1898 production

Herbert Beerbohm Tree's production at the end of the century was still within the nineteenth-century tradition of elaborate historical scenery, of 'upholstered Shakespeare', and of a star actor–manager who took the lead role. What would have surprised Kemble and Booth, however, and every other leading actor for the previous two hundred and fifty years, was that Tree did not take the role of Brutus, or even Cassius, but built his entire production around playing Mark Antony. This prominence given to Antony has continued in the twentieth century, notably in films (see p. 127)

This decision was almost certainly influenced by the visit of the private theatre company of the Duke of Saxe-Meiningen to England with *Julius Caesar* in 1881, almost the only production of the play in London for the thirty years up to Tree's revival. The Meiningen company's radical departure from tradition was to play as an ensemble rather than with star actors; thus, in *Julius Caesar*, a member of the mob in the Forum scene was as important as Brutus or Mark Antony. In the Forum scene the mob numbered several hundred, and far from being Booth's 'living scenery', they were all carefully rehearsed as individuals and small groups, and in their reactions to Brutus and Antony. For the first time the plebeians had become an integral part of the drama.

Tree saw how hard Antony had to work to persuade the mob, and the triumph of the actor when he succeeded. He therefore chose the role of Antony for himself, and trimmed the rest of the play to throw the focus his way. It was an actor's decision rather than a scholar's: writing to his wife he said, 'I like Brutus best – he is so much deeper – but I still feel that Antony has the colour – the glamour of the play, don't you?' Every time Antony was on stage Tree ensured he had business (e.g., 'laughing & talking with women', as the promptbook records in I.ii), and when he was offstage he hurried the action along. The Assassination scene was played quickly, and as butchery, until Antony's entrance: 'Then the silent, breathless, fearsome falling apart [of the conspirators] as the great figure of Marc Antony appeared, like a grim question silencing the heroics that died on guilty lips'. At the end of the scene, as he predicted civil war, Calpurnia came on to mourn the dead Caesar, and Antony had become not only the avenger of Caesar, but the widow's champion.

The Forum scene (III.ii) now had to replace the Assassination scene as the highpoint of the play. Initially Antony could not make himself heard, and overstepped the mark the first time he used sarcasm when referring to Brutus and the 'honourable men'. This crowd took real work to win over, but the payoff was an acting triumph for Tree.

The second half of the play seemed an anticlimax, of course, because the stature (and dramatic interest) of the conspirators, and the theme of liberty, had been so much reduced; 'Tree had demolished the traditional supremacy of Brutus and Cassius and the perennial popularity of their quarrel' (Ripley, p. 167).

A play of character: Shakespeare Memorial Theatre 1950

By the middle of the twentieth century, Shakespeare's text was accorded more respect than actor–managers such as Kemble, Booth, and Tree had shown. Directors would no longer write their own additional verse as Kemble had done, although cutting might still be drastic. At the Shakespeare Memorial Theatre in Stratford-upon-Avon, however, Anthony Quayle and Michael Langham presented *Julius Caesar* almost uncut. The Camp Poet episode and the second report of Portia's death (both in IV.ii) were the only significant cuts.

The aim of the production was evidently to present the characters as lifelike in what was now the accepted theatrical style of psychological realism, which had replaced the heightened idealism of the nineteenth century. At the same time, a sense of Roman grandeur was maintained by historical costuming, and by aspects of the design. Formal columns, arches, and steps in the first half declared the classical setting, although in fact the single-unit set was impressionistic and largely unchanging – an addition to a stage rather than a real place. This unlocalized quality encouraged rapid transition between scenes, and a fast pace to the production. At the end of II.ii, for instance, Caesar and the conspirators were still leaving the stage on one side as Artemidorus entered on the other reading his scroll.

Within this fast-moving action the concentration was on the major characters. Unusually for productions of *Julius Caesar*, Cassius got most attention. John Gielgud, one of Britain's leading classical actors, and a master of rhetorical control of Shakespearean verse, was uncertain of his suitability to play a martial character in Roman costume. Once famously described as having 'meaningless legs', Gielgud has himself said that with unprepossessing physiques in togas 'there is a danger of the effect of a lot of gentlemen sitting on marble benches in a Turkish bath' (Gielgud, p. 48). Critics, however, were in no doubt about his Cassius, including the battle scenes at the end. They found him ardent and impulsive, 'a fanatical crusader against totalitarianism' (Harold Conway, *Evening Standard*), and 'practical, opportunistic, vehement, and unscrupulous when the occasion demands' (Stephen Williams, *Evening News*). Cassius 'impels his colleagues to depose the dictator; and although he knows that Brutus is better built for leadership than himself, his restless temperament prods him to urgent pleading, fiery disagreement' (*Birmingham Post*). He was 'beyond question the most important person of every scene in which he figures' (*The Times*). Yet he also found sufficient nobility to justify Brutus's eulogy to 'the last of all the Romans' (V.iii.99). Fortunately, Gielgud's portrayal of Cassius in the 1953 film of the play is substantially that of this 1950 stage version, and therefore available to us still (see pp. 127–8).

Brutus (Harry Andrews) was by contrast gentle, quiet, dignified, sympathetic, his moral ascendency over his fellows never in doubt. Sympathy lay primarily with Brutus and Cassius, but essentially with the private human beings behind the public men. This focus on character brought the Quarrel scene (IV.ii), and Acts IV and V generally (the second half of this production, after the single interval) back into a prominence that had been lost by Tree in 1898, and those who followed him. Cassius' resigned acceptance of Brutus' mistaken military planning won him audience sympathy, and Brutus was the high-principled tragic liberal idealist that was increasingly the twentieth-century view of the failed politician.

Mark Antony was played by Anthony Quayle, who shared direction of the production with Michael Langham. Quayle was not afraid to show the unpleasant side of Antony's character, especially the hedonist ('Antony, that revels long a-nights', II.ii.116) and sycophant of the early scenes. And the Proscription scene (IV.i), always cut in the nineteenth century because of the callousness Antony displays, was now back in the play. Unlike Tree's Antony, Quayle's was one of a balanced set of characters in the play. The Forum scene (III.ii) was the major talking point, as the mob was 'a clamorous rabble . . . always a dangerous animal' (*The Times*). Antony responded with the roughest sort of oratory, often having to scream to make himself heard. He was 'half-politician, half-medium, a man possessed with the crowd's delirium. It is a striking performance. But the subtleties of the words themselves are lost. . . . That is the danger of naturalism in the staging of a Shakespearean crowd' (Richard Findlater, *Tribune*). Another critic found Quayle 'splendid', but also recognized that the Forum scene should be 'an intimate scene, however large the crowd, in the sense that it is a seduction scene' (*New Statesman*). Overall, 'Mark Antony's oration is showier; Brutus seizes our sympathy; Cassius rules' (J. C. Trewin, *John O'London's Weekly*).

And what of Caesar? As played by Andrew Cruikshank he was arrogant and surly, 'a cold, imperious, aging man' (*Warwick Advertiser*), a Caesar 'as unsympathetic as North's' (Alice Venezky, *Shakespeare Quarterly* 2 [1951], p. 74). Such a portrayal of course tended to make the conspirators more sympathetic, and also drew attention to the surprising devotion of the young Calpurnia to Caesar. The promptbook shows that Caesar's age (senility, according to some critics) or ill-health was emphasized by having him carried on in I.ii in a litter. Nevertheless, such a staging could also support 'majesty and distinction' of the character. Furthermore, the design made a strong statement about Caesar, 'IMPERATOR CAESAR' forming part of an inscription across the top of the colonnade that formed the setting for the first three acts. Caesar's name in stone – incontrovertible evidence of power.

Caesar was increasingly being regarded as a major factor in the meaning and unity of the play that bears his name. The production's graphic visual reminder of Caesar during the first half of the play in 1950, even when he was not on stage, was carried a step further in another Stratford production, in 1957. Here, the setting of huge ordered grey columns was synonymous with Caesar's importance to Rome:

> [T]he magnificence of the gold-embroidered crimson toga and the majesty of [Caesar's] bearing made him the incarnation of an immutable and pivotal principle of order. This ordered Rome was visible in the massive fluted monoliths of light grey stone, ranged outwards from Caesar as their personal centre in two symmetrical lines, continued in the tall stone portals flanking the fore-stage. Here was the wide perspective of Caesar's Rome with Caesar himself as the keystone.
>
> (Roy Walker, *Shakespeare Survey* 11 [1958], p. 132)

What the scenography here reinforced was a view of Caesar not as a tyrant to be destroyed by the forces of liberty, but 'the fount of authority' he would have been to the Elizabethans' (Humphreys, p. 68). When the pillars were disordered in the second half of the play, they symbolized the destruction that civil war had brought to Rome. And the lighting effect of a star carried the same message. As twilight darkened the Forum scene,

> the crowd, instead of being split into an awkward and distracting pattern of small character parts, merges into one impersonal rabble, growling from the dark. Behind all, one star glimmers. We find it too above the battlefield. Can it be the spirit of Caesar . . . ?'
>
> (J. C. Trewin, *Birmingham Post*)

Certainly when Brutus reacts to Cassius' death with 'O Julius Caesar, thou art mighty yet!' (V.iii.94), the star reappeared. Thus the setting and the star kept Caesar's presence alive right until the end. Nobody could cavil at the play being called in this production *Julius Caesar* rather than *The Tragedy of Brutus*, and politics was becoming crucial to its meaning.

Orson Welles and political Caesars

Orson Welles had first thrust contemporary politics to the fore in his now-legendary New York production at the Mercury Theatre in 1937. The impulse came from the deep dismay of American left-wing opinion at the growth during the 1920s and 1930s of fascist dictatorships in Italy and Germany. Publicity in fact subtitled the play, 'Death of a Dictator'. *Julius Caesar* was to be 'a political melodrama with clear contemporary parallels' (Houseman, *Run-through* , p. 298). Welles cut the text radically (the performance running just over an hour and a half) to emphasize only Caesar, Brutus, and the mob. He also caused a sensation by abandoning classical togas and military costume in favour of ordinary 1930s street clothes plus fascist uniforms. Dramatic shafts of light and pools of darkness, reminiscent of Hitler's night-time Nuremberg rally of 1937, sculpted the performers on the bare multi-level stage. Music reinforced an ominous sense of threat and of storm troopers on the march.

Despite inevitable simplification from severe cutting and such an overt political agenda, Welles set up what was to become one of the standard interpretations of the play: Brutus (whom he played himself) as 'the eternal, impotent, ineffectual, fumbling liberal. . . . the bourgeois intellectual, who, under a modern dictatorship would be the first to be put up against a wall and shot' (Welles, quoted in Ripley, p. 223). Set against this fatally idealistic Brutus was an arrogant uniformed Caesar wielding all the paraphernalia of the modern authoritarian state. Secret police and armed guards abounded, followers chanted and gave fascist salutes, and banners, music, and lighting were stage-managed to turn a mindless crowd into a vicious mob. The Cinna the Poet scene was presented for the first time ever in an American production, and came to typify for reviewers the success of Welles in warning of the immediate risks of allowing fascism to flourish. The understated, always reasonable, and principled Brutus was no match for the flood of violence and irrationality that his own action had inadvertently but inevitably instigated. Brutus and the conspirators were sympathetically portrayed, but doomed to failure because their liberalism was insufficiently ruthless to match the power they sought to remove.

Fascism and liberalism: RSC 1972

Trevor Nunn's 1972 Stratford production of Julius Caesar for the RSC (Royal Shakespeare Company) followed in the tradition of Welles, with Caesar dominant from the start. The play opened with an extra-textual procession prior to I.i: 'Amid brutal fanfares a red carpet unrolls down the rake and Caesar strides through a corridor of soldiers to face the audience' (Irving Wardle, *The Times*). Brutus then crowned Caesar with a laurel wreath as strictly regimented lines of senators and soldiers cried 'Hail, Caesar!' He arrived at the Capitol in III.i carried in an eagle-backed chair, a warlord and dictator with immense power. Anyone speaking to Caesar knelt to do so. There was nothing attractive about this sneering warlord: Michael Billington commented in the *Guardian* that 'not since Louis Calhern in the MGM movie [1953; see p. 127] have I seen a Caesar so ripe for assassination'.

Not only was Caesar powerful and unpleasant in himself, but clearly controlling the full apparatus of a fascist police state. The cries of 'Hail, Caesar!' were accompanied by the raised arm salute that twentieth-century dictators like Hitler and Mussolini modelled on classical Rome. The stage design was bare modernist marble, with banners and uniforms therefore dominant. Caesar and the soldiers were dressed in black armour, reminiscent of Mussolini's infamous blackshirts. The climate of fear and repressive authoritarianism was evident from the tribunes falling silent in I.i as two black-clad soldiers crossed the stage, and from soldiers closing in on the Soothsayer and, later, Artemidorus. This was 'no Rome of safety' (III.ii.289) for any democrat or liberal.

Caesar's position was symbolically reinforced by the inclusion of a massive statue of him dominating his house in II.ii, the only object on stage apart from his chair. The statue reappeared in IV.ii as his ghost, and then remained in the background during the battle sequences, bathed in blood-red light. Even more than in 1957, it was clear that Caesar had destroyed Republican Rome forever.

> It was implied by the production's emotional balance that Rome was well rid of Caesar, that Brutus' fastidious liberalism held no prospect of good government ... that Antony might have done much, but that the steely and utterly loveless Octavius would do more.
>
> (Peter Thomson, *Shakespeare Survey* 26 [1973], p. 145)

A fascist Caesar confronted by a weak, liberal Brutus, as a conscious allegory of twentieth-century political history, was directly in the tradition of Welles. The liberalism of Brutus, played by John Wood, was, for Michael Billington, 'the classic left-wing intellectual who wants revolution without bloodshed' (*Guardian*). This was, however, not the gentle nobility of Harry Andrews at Stratford in 1950, but a highly strung intellectual making a massive effort at self-control. Eric Shorter in the *Sunday Telegraph* felt emotionally distanced from the 'chilly, self-regarding portrait of a man to whom our hearts should go out'; the problem was that all Brutus' decisions came 'from a man whose faith in his power of reasoning is unshakeable' (John Mortimer, *Observer*). For several critics his introspection suggested a first draft by Shakespeare for Hamlet. But he failed to understand the hunger of others for emotional response.

Cassius (Patrick Stewart), by contrast, was full of fervour: with 'immense animal energy' he 'prods on the conspirators, his voice throbs, his eyes gleam with recollected excitements' (*Sunday Times*). At the assassination, whereas Brutus slashed Caesar's throat with one appalled movement, Cassius continued stabbing Caesar in a frenzy until Brutus eventually dragged him off. The Quarrel scene (IV.ii) was a highlight, Brutus's desperate self-control a constant goad to the emotional Cassius. Trevor Nunn, the director, reveals a telling example of Brutus' strength and weakness in this scene:

> Brutus himself questions his nobility. He questions himself and his own actions constantly. When at the height of the tent scene Brutus turns on Cassius and says, 'I shall be glad to learn of *noble* men', it's a vicious taunt at Cassius, but I also think it's an indication of the self-revulsion that is in him.... Cassius threatens Brutus, with 'I may do that I shall be sorry for' and Brutus replies, 'You have done that you should be sorry for.' That always seemed to us to be a paralysing moment. Brutus is talking about the assassination, and what Cassius has revealed of his motives. I am not saying that is unarguably the meaning of the line, but in performance it could only mean that one thing to the actors.
>
> (quoted in Berry, pp. 65–8)

Only at the end of the Quarrel scene did Brutus' sobs as he recounted the death of Portia reveal the deep feelings he nearly always kept repressed.

Politics, however, not personal feeling or characterization, was always at the centre of this production, in part because it was presented as part of a season of Roman plays alongside *Coriolanus*, *Antony and Cleopatra*, and *Titus Andronicus*. Although these plays are not a sequence, or even very closely akin to each other, the season was marketed as *The Romans*, and audiences were thereby encouraged to consider the social and political significance of Rome for Shakespeare. For *Julius Caesar*, the implications were most evident in foreshadowing *Antony and Cleopatra* as a sequel. Antony was in *Julius Caesar* the 'political adventurer rather than the reveller' (Irving Wardle, *The Times*), but he met his match in the cold Octavius. At the very end of the play Octavius interrupted Antony's eulogy over Brutus, and briskly exited to the right; Antony slowly shook his head and exited to the left. Nothing could be clearer as a prediction of continuation of the conflict in *Antony and Cleopatra*.

Promenade and politics: RSC 1993

David Thacker's 1993 production of *Julius Caesar* for the RSC at
Stratford, and subsequently on tour, was in The Other Place, a small,
makeshift 'black box' studio theatre. For this show, all seating was
removed from the main floor, so that most of the audience shared the
space with the actors, free to move around to follow the action, standing or sitting on the red carpet that covered the floor. Other audience
members chose seating in the gallery, but they too were on occasion
cheek by jowl with actors, who might suddenly pop up in any part of
the space. This 'promenade' style utterly broke down the usual conventional separation between actors and audience (whether proscenium
arch, stage height, or simply lighting); furthermore, the actor–audience
relationship was fluid and constantly changing. The appropriateness of
this design choice to the play caused real disagreement among critics,
as did the production's politics and the acting.

All critics commented on the promenade staging, and many were
enthusiastic. Russell Jackson, for instance, commented that 'promenading was very rewarding':

> In the private scenes it produced the sensation of being a privileged eaves-
> dropper, and the attention this commanded had a quality not often achieved
> in the theatre. In the public scenes the effect of a mass of citizens crowding
> in on Caesar's bier (or hospital trolley) or swayed by the orators would have
> been difficult to match in other theatres; so would the intimacy and indi-
> viduality of viewpoint that this staging conferred, for each member of the
> crowd saw things differently.
>
> (*Shakespeare Quarterly* 45 [1994], p. 339)

The production was immediate, with the actors very close, or appearing
unexpectedly from within the crowd making up the audience. Indeed,
part of the point was that the theatre audience actually became the
Roman crowd, and almost literally sheltered against the walls as the
mayhem of civil war erupted in their midst. 'All this creates a rare feeling of involvement and dramatic excitement,' said Charles Spencer, who
also noted that 'you actually experience what it feels like to be manipulated by a brilliant orator. . . . the audience has almost as important a part
to play as the cast' (*Daily Telegraph*). Other critics agreed that the biggest
payoff from the promenade staging was in the big public scenes, and

several noted the effect of Caesar's first entry being preceded by several large security or secret service men who created a lane for him through the real crowd, and, in this modern-dress production, the added focus of the shoulder-held television camera following his smiling progress. There was no shortage of extras in the Forum scene (III.ii), since the entire audience had become participants. For Paul Taylor this double-ness was a kind of theatrical magic: an audience 'that both merges with and is distinct from the Roman people whose feelings are so crucially manipulated and whipped up in the play' (*Independent*).

Approval, however, was not universal. Some critics who praised the excitement and immediacy also acknowledged that you might end up seeing only an actor's back at a crucial moment, or that an accidental boot from an actor running by during the battle would distract you from the play. Perhaps more intrusive on opening night was the sight of critics taking notes in the midst of the performance. But there were more significant criticisms. Several commentators found that the necessary shuffling around of the audience to get a reasonable view distracted attention from the intimate political scenes that are so important to the play. Others challenged the actor–audience relationship at a more fundamental level. Words like 'phoney' and 'spurious' were used to argue that the production's apparent immediacy and impact were no more than a meretricious and superficial substitute for the deeper issues of the play. The veteran critic Irving Wardle went further, and declared in the *Independent on Sunday* that 'promenading undoes the necessary division between spectator and event'. Michael Billington agreed, saying that, 'in the Forum, for instance, we become part of the crowd manipulated by Mark Antony's rhetoric instead of . . . objectively witnessing the table-turning anarchy and violence it unleashes'. Here was a critical debate that went wider than Shakespeare, that was indeed about the very nature of drama in performance. Yet it was also central to *Julius Caesar*, most especially in relation to the mob in III.ii.

A similar and related debate developed over the design and political ideology of the production. The immediacy sought by the promenade style was reinforced by modern dress and props: the conspirators in suits and ties in the Senate, Calpurnia gulping Scotch to calm herself after her nightmares, an officer feeding documents into a paper-shredder during the triumvirate's meeting (IV.i). This modernity was made more specific by the military uniforms and political banners. Although Caesar wore a suit in private, in public he wore a uniform jacket loaded with medals in the style of the former Soviet Union (which had collapsed only two years earlier) and its Eastern European satellites. Huge posters of Caesar on the walls suggested the propaganda of a totalitarian regime, as did banners with a Soviet-style star within a wreath, especially during III.i at the Capitol. Caesar himself, exactly like his image on the wall posters, appeared on a high platform at a lectern with microphone, television cameras, and spotlighting ready, backed by the full paraphernalia of a totalitarian state and security apparatus, with the audience staring up like a crowd at a political rally.

The programme reinforced this general effect by listing more than twenty countries that had suffered civil wars, uprisings, or a change of regime between 1985 and 1993. While no specific country was implied by the design, critics often found Romania called to mind (after Caesar's assassination the central star was ripped out of the banners just as the Soviet star had been torn from flags when the Romanians ousted Nicolae Ceauşescu). Others recalled the role of Boris Yeltsin in the collapse of the Soviet Union. And, in addition to these recent historical events, the civil wars and ethnic cleansing in the former Yugoslavia were on national television news every night; as Nicholas de Jongh put it, the promenade staging made 'Rome's civil war as close and shocking as the latest television pictures from Bosnia'. The camouflage uniforms of each side in the final stages of the play were indistinguishable, reflecting the appalling internecine nature of a 'civil war, with echoes of . . . Sarajevo . . . conveyed through smoke, a battery of machine guns, aerial attacks and flash fire. It graphically images Rome's ordered world rent asunder – and ours too' (*Evening Standard*).

Other critics, however, objected that the production obscured what Shakespeare makes clear in the battles: who is on which side. More significantly, they queried the dramaturgical results of the implied comparison of Caesar with various modern dictators.

> Coleridge spoke of the wonderful impartiality of Shakespeare's politics, and the play carefully balances the claims of Caesar and the conspirators. Ceausescu[*sic*] and the other East European dictators, however, had no claims on anyone's sympathy. . . .
>
> (Charles Spencer, *Daily Telegraph*)

Benedict Nightingale noted that 'the idea that somewhere in the world it is always about to be the Ides of March might count for more if the bringers of change were more trenchantly examined. After all, it is they, rather than Caesar, who fascinate Shakespeare' (*The Times*). Peter Holland added that *Julius Caesar* is 'a play far more uneasy about the manipulability of the mass of the people than I would like to be about the fall of Ceaucescu [*sic*] or the events of Tiananmen Square'. He went on to conclude that, despite appearances, 'Thacker's production was not one of the politics of ideology but of the human and hence corrupted nature of commitment, a commitment generated by individual psychology rather than political analysis' (Holland, p. 160).

'Individual psychology' brings us back, of course, to the acting of the major roles. The political centrality of dictatorship in the production concept meant that Caesar (David Sumner) was mentioned by critics at greater length than is common for this play. Several commented on his public image, constantly aware of his on-camera persona. 'The actor superbly captures the vacillating weakness of the inner man and the blandly smiling outer façade of the all-powerful demagogue' (Charles Spencer, *Daily Telegraph*). He was credible as a dictator, but not generally regarded as presenting the colossus of which Cassius warns Brutus.

The acting of Brutus divided critics almost as much as the production as a whole. For some he was a dignified and noble idealist. Paul Taylor also noted in the *Independent* that 'perhaps because he is black and has, in the past, been a fine Othello, Jeffery Kissoon as Brutus alerts you to the one similarity between the characters, that each needs to convince himself that an act of murder is not butchery but an elevated sacrifice'. For most critics, though, he was unconvincing, both physically and vocally. The word 'stolid' recurred. Alastair Macaulay asked in outrage, 'Can you believe that "the noblest Roman of them all" conspires Caesar's death with his hands in his pockets?' (*Financial Times*). His speech tended to remain on one level, with a resort to bombastic delivery at any moment of emotion.

Rob Edward's overstrung, slightly neurotic portrayal of Cassius was a complete contrast, attracting, as so often with this production, both praise and harsh criticism. Cassius's personal loathing of Caesar was startling, especially in the storm scene (I.iii), usually unremarked by reviewers, as he tore down a vast poster of the hated dictator. The Quarrel scene also was a high point, the stolid Brutus matched against the passionate Cassius with 'a simply desperate need to be loved by Brutus' (Holland, p. 161). The emotionalism of the performance was noted by nearly all critics, and may explain why those who were disappointed by Cassius struggled to explain why, and sought a variety of sometimes contradictory explanations.

The portrayal of Mark Antony raised less uncertainty, though more than one reviewer suggested that with his 'lean and hungry look' (I.ii.194) Barry Lynch might have been better cast as Cassius. He started the play appearing a lightweight, and was praised for the transition to a cunning avenger. He also took vocal advantage of the small theatre space in a way surprising for any Mark Antony, but characteristic of the entire production:

> [he] scores as a quiet, intense Antony, a whispering rabble-rouser. . . . The lynching of Cinna the poet might be the climax of an ugly riot on a London estate. Philippi might be happening in Bosnia tomorrow.
>
> (Benedict Nightingale, *The Times*)

5   The Play on Screen

Shakespeare Writing 'Julius Caesar' (1907), by the pioneer French filmmaker Georges Méliès, which includes in its ten-minute duration the assassination scene from the play, is one of the earliest screen versions of any Shakespeare; and the 1938 BBC *Julius Caesar* was the first full-length Shakespeare play ever broadcast on television. (The latter does not survive, of course, because television recording technology had not yet been invented.) Kenneth Rothwell lists fifteen screen versions of adaptations of the play altogether (Rothwell, pp. 342–3), of which the four most significant, all available on DVD or cassette, will be discussed here.

The first of the four was an American film directed by Northwestern University student David Bradley in 1950. Shot in black and white on 16mm, and with a budget of just $15,000, it was nevertheless an ambitious feature-length film. Its most notable success is in using local Chicago architecture – the massive neoclassical columns of a football stadium, the marble steps of a museum, the classical rotunda of a war memorial – to represent the grandeur of Rome. The actors are often deliberately dwarfed by colonnades and buildings, and the black and white cinematography makes expressive use of light and shadow. This scenic approach is an excellent example of the camera's ability to be selective in the service of both realism and atmosphere. The marble and columns are so impressive as to compel belief in the reality of the filmed world; but they are photographed so that nothing modern intrudes, and their grandeur therefore implies a monumental Rome that seems to overshadow (literally) the efforts of mere mortals to change the course of history and destiny.

The acting, almost entirely Northwestern University student amateurs (including the director himself as Brutus), is well spoken but uninspired, with the notable exception of the young Charlton Heston, himself a recent Northwestern graduate, and now a professional actor. His performance as Mark Antony provides a fascinating comparison with his playing of the same role twenty years later in the Burge film of 1970 (see below). Overall, however, the undistinguished acting, the heavy cutting, including all of the conspiracy in the Orchard scene (II.i), and the desperate shortage of actors to fill the vast architectural spaces, mean that the film is more significant as an essay in Shakespearean film-making than as a satisfying version of the play.

The most notable film of *Julius Caesar* appeared only three years later, in 1953, from MGM. The fact of its being a Hollywood studio production implied, at the time, that spectacle and known film stars would be essential, and that gross simplification of the play was likely. In the event, however, the producer and director (John Houseman and Joseph L. Mankiewicz), presented a remarkably intelligent and watchable version of the play which stands up well today despite being made over fifty years ago.

Spectacle there is, but serving the play. Roman sets from the recent epic film *Quo Vadis* were re-used, but stripped of their ornamentation. Ancient Rome is presented not in its Imperial splendour as the nineteenth-century theatre had done (see pp. 109–13), but as an expanding city full of scaffolding and half-completed buildings. The architecture is grand, but full of unexpected stairways and turnings, so that characters can find small spaces to be alone in the midst of the grandeur (for instance, Cassius and Brutus in I.ii; though, ironically, busts of Caesar overlook their private talk).

The Hollywood budget allowed for a cast of thousands when required, and the Forum scene and the battles are spectacular in a way that expands on what the nineteenth-century theatre presented as historical realism. At its best the spectacle, supported by an impressive musical score, can persuade us that this is how the events must have looked and happened. Only occasionally do the conventions of Hollywood spectacle become intrusive, as when the final battle follows the hackneyed movie conventions of ambush in a dry arroyo already familiar from many, many westerns. Overall, however, restraint is evident, and spectacle seldom used for its own sake.

Further restraint was evident in the decision to resist MGM demands for shooting in colour. Just as Laurence Olivier chose black and white for his film of *Hamlet* in 1948 (despite having used colour for *Henry V* in 1944), so Houseman and Mankiewicz made the artistic decision for black and white as more appropriate than colour for the tragic events of *Julius Caesar*. This was to be drama rather than epic. Furthermore, black and white might remind audiences of World War II newsreels, carrying an implication of historical authenticity.

Star actors were cast in the leading roles, but again there were surprises. John Gielgud, a leading British stage actor rather than an American Hollywood star, was cast as Cassius, repeating the furious eloquence of his recent success in the role at Stratford in 1950 (see p. 114). Furthermore, the director resisted the common film temptation to drastically cut Shakespeare's rhetorical speeches, so that we can today absorb not only Gielgud's Cassius in the film, but also his likely impact in his famous stage portrayal. Cast opposite Gielgud's classicism was an established realist actor, James Mason. Mason's Brutus is quiet, aloof, a sensitive and introspective liberal. Caesar, the man they must kill, is the imposing Louis Calhern, a towering six foot five inch (195 cm.) dictator. When the bloody and badly wounded Caesar crosses the floor towards Brutus, the camera lingers on Brutus' horrified face, stricken not only by the brutality he has unleashed, but by his duty now to contribute 'the most unkindest cut of all' (III.ii.180); this was a suffering Brutus in the tradition of Edwin Booth (see pp. 108–12).

The most daring casting decision, given the experience of these three actors, was to cast as Antony the young Method actor Marlon Brando. Brando was best known for his recent stage role as the Polish redneck Stanley Kowalski in *Streetcar Named Desire*, famous for his slurred naturalist speech, slouching posture, and 'tough-guy' appearance. Although controversy raged both before and after release of the film about his appropriateness to play a Shakespearean role, and the quality of his verse speaking, there is no question now but that both his vocal clarity (assisted in rehearsal, apparently, by Gielgud) and the intensity of his muscular physical presence render him a powerful counter to Brutus and Cassius (compare Tree in 1898, pp. 112–13). The Forum scene (III.ii) is carefully orchestrated to present both Antony's rhetorical manipulation of the crowd and a compelling inner characterization.

Actors and language were well served by Mankiewicz's decision to sharply reduce the then-standard use of 'reaction shots' when one character is talking to another; instead, he decided that the rhythm and length of the speech should determine how long the camera remained on the speaker. Although not obvious except through careful comparison with other Hollywood movies of the time, the editing of *Julius Caesar* marks a breakthrough in film interpretation of Shakespeare.

Furthermore, the producer and director were eager to suggest a historical parallel between Caesar's Rome and the rise of fascism in Europe leading to World War II. The opening credits of the film show a Roman eagle that looks very similar to the Nazi version of the German eagle, and the black and white, it was hoped, might evoke newsreel images of

Mussolini and Hitler. Similarly, the two anti-Caesar tribunes have no sooner finished haranguing the crowd at the end of I.i than watchful centurions step forward and escort them away; they have been 'put to silence' (I.ii.282–3) as if by Hitler's Gestapo or Stalin's secret police. (An alternative political reading might see the film in terms of the McCarthyist Cold War anti-communism of the early 1950s in the US, with a British Cassius as suspect, and Brutus as either idealistic democrat or liberal dupe.)

None of this is imposed on the film in a programmatic way, however. Shakespeare's Roman story is played out with a balance of strength and complexity in each of the four main characters. The passionate Cassius persuades the high-minded Brutus to action; the charismatic Antony deliberately sits in Caesar's chair as he picks up the reins of power from the physically imposing but fundamentally weak dictator after the assassination. In addition, the black and white cinematography is used expressionistically on occasion, especially early in the play to empha-size the effect of the fearful storm in Acts I and II on the minds and spir-its of the conspirators, and on Caesar and his wife. Patterns of light and shade in the Orchard scene (II.i), for instance, imply the disturbance in Brutus' mind. Calpurnia (Greer Garson) is also used to strengthen a sense of fatality and doom when she is shown retiring from Caesar's presence as he prepares to leave for the Capitol, and closing the doors behind her in a tragic way that assures us of her certainty of Caesar's (and her own) impending destruction.

At the other end of critical reception was the 1970 film directed by Stuart Burge. 'As flat and juiceless as a dead haddock' (*New York Times*) was the general verdict, but its failure 'remains one of the great myster-ies in the history of filmed Shakespeare. Presumably it had everything going for it – professional direction, an excellent cast, intelligent script' (Rothwell, p. 153). Much of the problem lies with the passionless acting of Jason Robards, who apparently decided to play Brutus as an intellec-tual suppressing his emotions, and succeeded so well as to deprive him of all interest. The RSC-trained Richard Johnson as Cassius is more per-suasive, but has little to play against. John Gielgud can be seen again, this time as a vain and fastidious Caesar, utterly unlike his 1953 Cassius. Once Caesar is dead, Charlton Heston's Antony takes over the film, not just in acting, but also in directorial choices: Antony is much more relaxed than Octavius during the battles, as well as a more swashbuck-ling fighter, and cutting Octavius' final speech gives a detached and cynical Antony the last word. Heston is rumoured to have funded the film, and if so his dominance should be no more surprising than that of Tree in 1898 (see pp. 112–13).

The final screen version of *Julius Caesar* to be considered here is the BBC television version that in 1979 kicked off the ambitious series that would over the next few years record all Shakespeare's plays for the small screen. Any film enthusiast coming to it for the first time tends to be deeply disappointed, criticizing it for its small cast, lacklustre studio sets, lack of Roman spectacle, and dull televisual camera work: limited camera movement, low definition visuals, lack of variety in camera angle and shot choice, monotonous reliance on slow zooms and a succession of close-ups.

None of this is surprising, since television in general developed from radio, and therefore has always, for institutional as well as technological reasons, emphasized language and acting, whereas film grew from photography, and has always placed high value on the visual image. Furthermore, the BBC *Julius Caesar* was part of the initial two-year period during which the series producer, Cedric Messina, established a cautious 'house style'. Directors (in this case, Herbert Wise) were to adopt a realist approach to the plays, to avoid design or directorial gimmicks or conceptual interpretation, to 'let the plays speak for themselves'. As is clear from the discussion elsewhere in this book (see especially Key Productions and Performances, and the Commentary), a play can never speak for itself; it is spoken and lived by actors who make a multitude of specific intellectual, emotional, and physical decisions in performance. More recently directors, designers, and others who create patterns and contexts within which actors and audience operate have added their contribution. So 'straight' productions of Shakespeare, such as Messina sought, will always be in danger of lacking the imaginative interpretation that brings Shakespeare alive.

But although this *Julius Caesar* lacks the kind of visual excitement offered by most feature films made for cinema release, Shakespeare scholars and others familiar with the play have often praised it for its uncomplicated presentation of an almost full-text version of the play. (All other screen versions have made significant cuts.) Furthermore, they respond to the clarity of the speech, and to the intelligence of the acting. What the production lacks in spectacle and visual excitement it makes up for by exploring in private close-up the actors of this most public of stories. The choice to watch this TV version, therefore, may hinge on how serious the viewer is about pondering the meaning of the play, and how willing to make serious comparisons with other productions.

Such comparisons can be instructive. For instance, the BBC Caesar, played by Charles Grey, on his return in I.ii after having refused the crown suddenly totters and needs Antony's support on the stairs; but then immediately displays a vanity that refuses such support, and draws himself up as if the moment of physical weakness had never occurred. Yet in III.i, when he is first stabbed, he turns and starts to fight off Casca, only being subdued by subsequent thrusts. In the Mankiewicz film of 1953, and even more in the Burge film of 1970, the Caesars are more physically fit, but at the moment of assassination they do not fight back: they are acted and filmed from the start as victims.

A more complex difference between the BBC and Mankiewicz versions may be observed by focusing on the immediate aftermath of the assassination. It is often difficult when watching any performance, stage or screen, to notice where cuts have been made. One cut in the Mankiewicz version is a short section after Brutus says 'Stoop, Romans, stoop, / And let us bathe our hands in Caesar's blood' (III.i.105–6):

> Up to the elbows, and besmear our swords.
> Then walk we forth, even to the market-place,
> And waving our red weapons o'er our heads,
> Let's all cry 'Peace, freedom, and liberty!'
> CASSIUS Stoop, then, and wash.
>
> (III.i.107–11)

Cutting these lines reduces emphasis on the bloody implications of the ritual, and on possible audience recollection of Brutus' earlier desire that the conspirators 'be sacrificers, but not butchers' (II.i.167). Furthermore, the black and white of the Mankiewicz film also reduces the potential visceral shock of the blood. The BBC version contrasts sharply with this: the lines are retained, Richard Pasco's Brutus invokes a ritual aspect to the bathing with blood by holding both arms aloft as he speaks before and after smearing himself, and the glistening red blood is so plentiful on both weapons and hands of the conspirators that Antony's hand is stained red by shaking hands with them (and is still bloody during his Forum speech to the crowd). The one approach tends to make easier an acceptance of the nobility of Brutus and the conspirators, whereas the fuller BBC version poses more complex questions about the contradictions inherent in trying to distinguish between carving 'a dish fit for the gods' and hewing 'a carcass fit for hounds' (II.i.174–5; and see pp. 1–2).

A final example of how different the interpretative choices may be from the same text can be seen by comparing the Quarrel scene (IV.ii) in the Mankiewicz and BBC versions. The Mankiewicz film allows John Gielgud's Cassius to be the angry wave crashing against the stoic rock of Brutus, whereas in the television version Pasco's Brutus is much the angrier figure. A fascinating comparison itself in terms of interpreting text into action, the directorial and acting decisions are also of no small importance for the balance of the entire play, and especially for the way in which the audience regards Brutus as the results of assassinating Caesar combine against him at the end.

6   Critical Assessments

Early criticism

The enthusiasm of Thomas Platter and Leonard Digges for early performances of *Julius Caesar* (see pp. 2, 7) was countered at the end of
the seventeenth century by Thomas Rymer and John Dennis, who
criticized Shakespeare's failure to live up to neoclassical rules of how
to write tragedy. Both felt that the grandeur of Rome and neoclassical purity of tragedy were insufficiently respected: 'Caesar and *Brutus* . . .
put in Fools Coats, and [made] Jack-puddens' (Rymer, 1693), and the
depiction of 'the Rabble in *Julius Caesar*' offending against 'the Dignity of that noble Poem' (Dennis, 1711). Dennis also wondered how
Shakespeare 'could have made so very little of the first and greatest of
Men, as that *Caesar* should be but a Fourth-rate Actor in his own Tragedy?'
The answer was that throughout the eighteenth and nineteenth centuries
Brutus was regarded as the hero. And eighteenth-century heavyweights
such as Pope and Johnson defended Shakespeare's accuracy in delineat-
ing ancient Rome: 'In . . . *Julius Caesar*, not only the Spirit, but Manners,
of the *Romans* are exactly drawn' (Pope, 1725). Already some of the major
critical issues were being identified: the relationship of the play to Roman
history, Shakespeare's treatment of leading characters, and the structure
of a play named after a character who is killed early in Act III.

In the nineteenth century Romantic criticism superseded the
neoclassical rules; greatness of soul and intensity of suffering
assumed new importance. And William Hazlitt, writing in 1817,
responded to the play as if it were a historical document: 'It is as
if [Shakespeare] had actually been present, had known the different characters and what they thought of one another, and had taken
down what he heard and saw, their looks, words, and gestures, just as
they happened'. He goes on to praise Shakespeare for his 'profound
knowledge of character', commenting acutely on the difference
between Brutus and Cassius:

[T]he whole design of the conspirators to liberate their country fails from the generous temper and overweening confidence of Brutus in the goodness of their cause and the assistance of others. Thus it has always been. Those who mean well themselves think well of others. . . . Cassius was better cut out for a conspirator. . . . His watchful jealousy made him fear the worst that might happen. . . . The mixed nature of his motives made him fitter to contend with bad men.

(Hazlitt, p. 198)

Twentieth-century criticism

A.C. Bradley's work marks the beginning of modern criticism of Shakespeare, and his most lasting legacy has been a critical concentration on character. Although his landmark book *Shakespearean Tragedy* (1904) is principally devoted to *Hamlet, Othello, King Lear,* and *Macbeth,* Bradley often uses *Julius Caesar* for comparison in his introductory chapters on the nature and construction of Shakespeare's tragedies. A tragedy, he says, is above all the story of one person, the 'hero', and he immediately notes that '*Julius Caesar* is not an exception to this rule. Caesar, whose murder comes in the Third Act, is in a sense the dominating figure in the story, but Brutus is the "hero"' (Bradley, p. 2). This view of Brutus, of course, continues a 200-year tradition. But for Bradley, character drives tragedy, and his focus derives largely from nineteenth-century developments in the realist novel, criticism, and psychology. He is particularly interested in *Julius Caesar,* written just before *Hamlet,* as the play in which Shakespeare's interest moved sharply towards the inward struggle within the tragic hero, the hallmark of his mature work. Both plays, he says, may be regarded as 'tragedy of thought' (Bradley, p. 63), rather than about a hero with an undivided soul.

Although Bradley has been criticized for excessive concentration on character, he is also concerned with structure:

> Shakespeare's general plan, we have seen, is to show one set of forces advancing, in secret or open opposition to the other, to some decisive success, and then driven downward to defeat by the reaction it provokes. And the advantages of this plan, as seen in such a typical instance as *Julius Caesar,* are manifest. It conveys the movement of the conflict to the mind with great clearness and force. It helps to produce the impression that in his decline and fall the doer's act is returning on his own head. And, finally, as used by Shakespeare, it makes the first half of the play intensely interesting and dramatic.

* * *

> The quarrel-scene illustrates yet another favourite expedient. In this section of a tragedy Shakespeare often appeals to an emotion different from any of those excited in the first half of the play, and so provides novelty and generally also relief.
>
> (Bradley, pp. 42, 46)

But Bradley is far from merely setting out mechanical structures; for him, tragedy is a painful mystery, and he sees the struggle of the virtuous Brutus with the evil he unleashes as needing to be intensely experienced as well as carefully analysed.

Intense experience of the play is also central to G. Wilson Knight, who acknowledges his criticism as following in a direct line from Bradley. Knight, too, concentrates on the main characters of *Julius Caesar*, but he is principally interested in the thematic structure of the play as uncovered by a detailed attention to imagery. Whereas Caroline Spurgeon, who was to popularize 'image clusters' as a critical tool, finds *Julius Caesar* 'restrained, almost bare in style; it has relatively few images' (Spurgeon, p. 346), Knight in 1931 responded passionately to the same evidence:

> 'Love' is everywhere important. Our vision has wider significances than those of physique: it sees through the body to the spirit. . . . 'heart', 'spirit', 'fire': to those I now pass, and to the theme of the body (Caesar's, and in a wider sense, Rome's) broken, gashed, loosing streams of rich life-blood, fountains of life's elixir. 'Blood', too, is here lovingly, almost erotically described: 'blood', and the 'heart' whose life it feeds, this blending with 'passion' and 'emotion'.
>
> (Knight, *The Imperial Theme*, pp. 44–5)

Knight's poetic but meticulously detailed vision of the play sees Antony's love for Caesar as finally healing the wounds of Caesar's death unleashed by the Republic-loving Cassius and the honourable Brutus who suppresses love. Caesar is seen in two aspects: weak physical man, and spirit, idea, symbol. Thus without displacing Brutus as the hero, Caesar is brought to critical centrality because his death is the thematic catalyst of the play. In addition, Knight urges us to 'cut below the surface crust of plot and "character", and to expose [the] riches of poetic imagination' (Knight, *The Wheel of Fire*, p. 132). He identifies for the first time remarkable parallels between Brutus and Macbeth; not ethical parallels, of course, but what he called the similar poetic situation of both men, inwardly deeply divided:

Brutus...is twined in the meshes of the immediately actual and impending...
murder, and yet sees all the time its essential breaking of the natural
evolved laws of humanity. It is this twofold consciousness of the unnatural
within the actual that creates disorder in the soul of Brutus and Macbeth.
And we . . . feel a similar symbolic disorder within the order of nature. Thus
the poetic symbolism forces us to see the central act of *Julius Caesar* more
nearly through the vision of a Brutus that that of any other of the chief
persons.

(Knight, *The Wheel of Fire*, p. 150)

From this time on, criticism of *Julius Caesar* became much more various. Far more attention was now paid to theme and structure. Nevertheless, the central characters inevitably remained a continuing source
of critical attention. Scholars like Mark Hunter and T. S. Dorsch argue
against an over-idealized view of Brutus, and emphasize the greatness
of Caesar, whereas J. Dover Wilson (whose edition appeared in the aftermath of the defeat of Hitler in World War II) depicts Caesar and 'Caesarism' as utterly tyrannical: 'the Caesar who falls on Shakespeare's Capitol
is the universal Dictator' (Wilson, p. xxxiii). Ernest Schanzer complicates
matters further by arguing that both attitudes to Caesar are deliberately
deployed by Shakespeare in such a manner that an ambivalent reaction
is inevitable. He accepts that 'on our view of Caesar depends, very largely,
our judgement of the justifiability of the entire conspiracy', and argues
that, because audience views will be 'varied and divided', *Julius Caesar* is a
'problem play' (Schanzer, p. 33). Schanzer bolsters his case with a detailed
examination of how Shakespeare marshalled the pro- and anti-Caesar
attitudes in the wide variety of classical sources with which he would
have been at least generally familiar. This close attention to classical
Rome was becoming increasingly important in critical reaction.

The idea of Rome

Modern translations of Plutarch became available from the late
nineteenth century, and editions of the selections Shakespeare used
from the early twentieth century. Serious attention to Shakespeare's
use and understanding of Plutarch started with M. W. MacCallum's
weighty *Shakespeare's Roman Plays* in 1910, and was significantly
sharpened by T. J. B. Spencer's influential 1957 article 'Shakespeare
and the Elizabethan Romans'. Spencer not only went back to the
classical texts, but also looked carefully at which were most known

(and translated) in Elizabethan England. While writers like Suetonius and Tacitus could be demonstrated to be Imperial in their bias compared to the generally Republican Plutarch, it was perhaps more important that the political and moral debate around the assassination of Caesar was the source of as much debate in classical times as it has been since. Geoffrey Bullough's monumental *Narrative and Dramatic Sources of Shakespeare* made easily available the range of sources Shakespeare may have used.

Expanding those sources to include Virgil's *Aeneid*, Robert S. Miola also takes Rome itself to be an important element of Shakespeare's vision:

> Constructed of forums, walls, and Capitol, opposed to outlying battlefields, wild, primitive landscapes, and enemy cities, Rome is a palpable though ever-changing presence. The city serves not only as a setting for action, but also as central protagonist.
>
> (Miola, *Shakespeare's Rome*, p. 17)

Miola emphasizes three Roman ideals in particular: constancy, honour, and *pietas*. Geoffrey Miles, in *Shakespeare and the Constant Romans* (1996), makes a special study of constancy as a Roman Stoic virtue, taking as his starting point Brutus' lines urging the conspirators to

> ... bear it as our Roman actors do,
> With untired spirits and formal constancy.
>   (II.i.227–8)

The reference to 'Roman actors' suggests that 'formal constancy', consistent decorum, resembles stage acting in that a certain external image must be maintained. Just as Schanzer propounded a dualistic Caesar, so Miles sees Brutus as having to suppress his emotions in order to act the noble role in which he sees himself as others see him. Brutus receives the second report of Portia's death, from Messala (see p. 9), with great stoicism, seeming to have no knowledge of her death:

> Why, farewell, Portia. We must die, Messala.
> With meditating that she must die once,
> I have the patience to endure it now.
>   (IV.ii.240–2)

Cassius responds:

> I have as much of this in art as you,
> But yet my nature could not bear it so.
> (IV.ii.244–5)

Miles's comment on this is worth quoting at length:

> In this public response Brutus is . . . maintaining decorum, the behaviour
> appropriate to 'a Roman' and to Brutus. . . . But in the process of maintaining
> formal constancy he is forced to dissemble his true feelings and tell a flat lie.
> The ambiguity of Cassius' half-admiring, half-appalled comment hinges on
> the meaning of 'art'. Its primary, ostensible meaning is . . . 'I am as well trained
> as you in Stoic ethical theory, but I couldn't bear to put it into practice like
> this.' There is, however, a secondary meaning shared only between Cassius
> and Brutus . . . 'I thought *I* was a good hypocrite, but how can you bear to act
> at a moment like this?' Many critics, equally appalled, have explained away
> the duplicate revelation as a confusion produced by rewriting. I see it rather
> as central to Shakespeare's portrayal of constancy: as a genuinely noble
> ideal which nevertheless rests on unnatural suppression of feeling and on
> 'artful' pretence, both directed toward satisfying the opinions of others.
>
> (Miles, p. 145)

'Only in death' says Miles, discussing the suicide of Brutus, 'can he end
the strain of pretence, and achieve . . . a complete identification between
himself and his public role' (Miles, p. 148).

Suicide is an essential component of 'constancy', and central to the
specifically Roman quality of *Julius Caesar*. As Clifford Ronan says,

> The conspirators kill themselves in the same way that they killed Caesar:
> with a clear awareness of spectators, of an audience – of the Roman Senate
> and People, or the world of spirits and gods, and of posterity, even those in
> 'States unborn, and accents yet unknown'.
>
> (Ronan, p. 95)

Quoting Titinius' line as he prepares to commit suicide, 'By your leave,
gods; this is a Roman's part' (V.iii.89), Ronan notes that 'Titinius recognizes that his act is probably ungodly but excuses it on "a Roman's
cultural grounds"' (Ronan, p. 95). Suicide is just one of many identi-
fiably 'Roman' characteristics, but Ronan here draws attention to the
Elizabethan Christian audiences who would have found it 'ungodly';
indeed categorically sinful. Much of the criticism focused on Rome

has, of necessity, been equally concerned with what Rome meant in England at the end of the sixteenth century.

The idea of England

Like Ronan, Robert S. Miola draws attention not just to classical depictions of Rome, but also to the use Shakespeare makes of classical history and knowledge in his own time. Elizabeth's reign was clearly drawing to an end, a reign in which religious and political controversy had raged. Debate over the basis of sovereignty, and even over the legitimacy of challenging the authority of an earthly monarch, was no academic abstraction; Elizabeth had faced the threat of foreign invasion, domestic plotting, and even of assassination. Her famous comment, 'Know you not that I am Richard II', indicates her knowledge that an event from history – such as the deposition of a monarch – might be recycled so as to point towards her. Miola usefully examines the late sixteenth-century understanding of the tyrannicide debate, and Shakespeare's use of it. Caesar's death was central to the debate, since it could be argued whether or not he was, or would have become, a tyrant; and also whether or not the conspirators met the tests of legitimate tyrannicide. Miola demonstrates how strongly Renaissance opinions might diverge:

> Salutati, for example, praised Caesar as 'the father of his country, the lawful and benignant ruler of the world'. . . . Suarez, however, condemned Caesar as a usurper of sovereign power 'through violence and tyranny'. . . . This debate defined precisely those questions important to the play: how to tell a tyrant from a just king; how to tell envious murderers from heroic republicans; how and when to justify assassination.
>
> (Miola, '*Julius Caesar* and the Tyrannicide Debate', pp. 272–3)

Miola's work, like that of Ronan, Miles, and Spencer, brings a new precision to our understanding of how the Elizabethans understood Rome. Sharing Miola's belief that Shakespeare's anachronisms are both complex and often intentional, Sigurd Burckhardt's article 'How Not to Murder Caesar' starts with the clock that strikes three in the Orchard scene (II.i). Agreeing that it is an anachronism, Burckhardt explores what it might signify if Shakespeare put it into the play deliberately. This leads him to uncertainties expressed elsewhere in the scene about the time of day, month, and year. With this attention to difficulties with time, he suggests that the Folio reading, 'Is not tomorrow, boy, the first of March?' (II.i.40; usually emended to 'Ides of March', the fifteenth) is explicitly drawing attention to the Julian calendar on which Caesar's fame in early modern Europe partly rested. More important, however, is that in this reading Brutus is out by fifteen days, an error that Burckhardt argues is clearly drawing attention to the 1582 reform of the Julian calendar: a reform operative in Catholic countries but not in England. Thus 'a situation existed in Europe exactly analogous to that of Rome in 44 BC. It was a time of confusion and uncertainty, when the most basic category by which men order their experience seemed to have become unstable and untrustworthy, subject to arbitrary political manipulation' (Burckhardt, p. 6). Whether or not one accepts the argument, it is a forceful statement of the need to pay close attention to the social context within which Shakespeare was writing, and the audience for whom he was writing.

Steve Sohmer, in *Shakespeare's Mystery Play* (1999), attempts to narrow both the calendar argument and the timetable for opening the new Globe Theatre to demonstrate that Shakespeare was not only writing for the known opening date, but has incorporated the Christian liturgical calendar as well as the Julian calendar. This attention to Christianity is a useful extension of the purely Roman research on sacrifice and religion.

Modern schools of criticism

Critical theory has in recent years developed in a number of new directions, although some of them have long antecedents. It will be worth looking at several modern 'schools' of criticism in relation to *Julius Caesar*: in particular Materialist Criticism, Feminist and Gender Criticism, and Theatrical Criticism.

Materialist criticism

Sometimes known as New Historicism (especially in the US) or Cultural Materialism (especially in Britain, and more Marxist in orientation), materialist criticism is concerned with confronting an older critical view of artistic genius as universal: as transcending the time and place of composition. Rather, materialist Shakespeare critics stress the material circumstances of the writer's life and work, of writing, performing, and publishing, and the ideologies of politics, economics, gender and other material conditions. Often historical anecdote is used as a way of opening up a new sense of historicity for the modern reader. In addition, the left-wing stance of the critic is evident; much of the research is explicitly designed to demonstrate subversive and anti-authoritarian elements within the play.

Richard Wilson, for instance, takes the opening lines of the play as drawing on the entertainments on Bankside (including the new Globe Theatre itself) as lures for working men who had no business being on 'holiday' (I.i.2).

> The first words uttered on the stage of the Globe can be interpreted, then, as a manoeuvre in the campaign to legitimise the Shakespearean stage and dissociate it from the subversiveness of London's artisanal subculture.... The Shakespearean text belongs to a historical moment when a revolutionary bourgeois politics has not yet naturalised its own repressive procedures, and Brutus's Machiavellian realpolitik is a complete statement of the technique of the modern state whereby subversion is produced in both consciousness and society to legitimise the order that subjects it. Unruly passions and apprentices are both checked by a regime that contrives to 'Stir up the ... youth to merriments' the better to invigilate it.
>
> (Wilson, 'Is This a Holiday?', pp. 47–9)

In other words, when Brutus urges the conspirators to

> ... let our hearts, as subtle masters do,
> Stir up their servants to an act of rage
> And after seem to chide 'em.
>   (II.i.176–8)

he is recommending that they be *agents provocateurs*, just as the 'modern state' will promote subversion in order to justify an aggregation of state power to control that and any other subversion. Wilson seems to be arguing that on the one hand the Globe Theatre as a commercial enterprise is being co-opted by an emergent bourgeois ideology, while at the same time Shakespeare's play is subversively revealing the power play of which it is a part. In these terms Caesar becomes a Lord of Misrule from the medieval life-giving carnival tradition, while the tribunes in the first scene of the play are Puritan precursors of the English Civil War in the seventeenth century, and of the rise of capitalist social control after the Industrial Revolution and into the modern age of mass consumption.

Catherine Belsey is less programmatic in her approach, but equally concerned with power, and the way in which representations of Rome might offer an indirect way of talking about forbidden topics of Elizabethan politics:

> [O]ccasionally, as in *Julius Caesar*, tyranny and sedition are brought into confrontation, with the effect of raising the . . . question of freedom. Roman history, by contrasting the liberty of the Republic with Imperial tyranny, introduced into the range of what it was possible to consider the third model of political organization which absolutist propaganda, based on antithesis, effaced. The Roman Republic in its Renaissance representation was to all intents and purposes a democracy. . . . It does not (cannot in 1599?) choose decisively between them, but it offers its audience the opportunity to reflect on the differences.
>
> (Belsey, pp. 101–2)

The year in which *Julius Caesar* was written and first performed, 1599, was an eventful year, not least for Shakespeare's theatre company opening their new theatre the Globe, possibly with this very play. James Shapiro's book *1599* is a highly readable biography of Shakespeare during this year, and its historicism is its strength. Without imposing a definite interpretation on what we can never know – what Shakespeare was thinking – it provides a persuasive account of events current and discussed during the year, and the topics that might have interested Shakespeare as he prepared *Julius Caesar* and his following play, *Hamlet*. The war in Ireland and Essex's return to challenge Elizabeth's authority, assassination plots against the queen, religious controversy, accusations of tyranny, the growing anxiety about Elizabeth's successor; these are subjects around which debate and gossip swirled. Shapiro is alert also to the London images that may have sprung to Shakespeare's mind when he read Plutarch:

> On 17 and 18 November, a Saturday and Sunday, Hugh Holland and John Richardson preached back-to-back sermons at Paul's Cross pulpit. If the public theatres could hold upwards of 3,000 spectators, the crowded outdoor space around the raised pulpit outside St Paul's Cathedral could hold twice that number. When Brutus and Antony take turns speaking at the open-air 'pulpit' in *Julius Caesar*, it is just such a site that Shakespeare and his audience would have had in mind. . . . The crowd, alert to 'bugswords' or coded language, got the point and news quickly spread that Richardson, 'in open pulpit, spoke much of the misgovernment in Ireland; and used many words of the duty of subjects to their princes'.
>
> (Shapiro, pp. 188–9)

A recent book by Lisa Hopkins, though principally dealing with the period following the death of Elizabeth, notes the large number of references in other plays to Julius Caesar as 'the paradigmatic Roman', and discusses the way in which Shakespeare's *Julius Caesar* and *Hamlet* engage with the classical question of whether or not violence should be shown on stage:

> In doing so, I think, it offers both an implicit criticism of the incoming James VI and I . . . and a declaration of solidarity with the collective cultural enterprise of the early modern stage, which, unlike its Roman predecessor, did not shrink from the overt use of violence to explore the issues it wished to address.
>
> (Hopkins, p. 54)

Feminist and gender criticism

Although much of the specifically Shakespearean feminist criticism since its modern emergence in the 1970s has been concerned with gender relations in the romantic comedies, a number of critics, including Catherine Belsey (see above), have addressed themselves to the tragedies, and to the way in which Shakespeare may be seen as traditionally patriarchal, radically proto-feminist, conservatively heterosexual, subversively bisexual, or any of a number of alternatives. As significantly, a feminist perspective serves to interrogate much previous (male) criticism for often unconscious but nonetheless significant blindness to issues of gender.

Gail Kern Paster, for instance, suggests that Portia's 'voluntary wound' is 'Here, in the thigh' (II.i.301–2) 'not to remind Brutus of her femaleness, her lack of the phallus, but rather to offer the wound as substitute phallus. Hers is not the involuntary wound of the leaking female body but the honorifically gendered, purgative, *voluntary* wound of the male.' She goes on to argue that by asserting a masculine wounding and bleeding she 'furthers the conspirators' ideological project of regendering Caesar' (Paster, p. 294). And Caesar, paradoxically feminized by his wounds and involuntary bleeding, is available to be exploited by Antony, whose image of 'put[ting] a tongue / In every wound of Caesar' (III.ii.221–2) 'seems to oppose femaleness with a phallicized image of speech. . . . By fetishizing [the wounds] to the crowd, Antony can eroticize "sweet" Caesar's female woundedness as the explicit motive of his rhetorical power. . . .' (Paster, pp. 297–8).

Whereas Paster's insistent sexualizing makes the conspirators' 'ideological project of regendering Caesar' almost conscious, Coppélia Kahn interprets what the conspirators are doing in terms of a wider analysis of Rome as itself gendered:

> In Rome and in Shakespeare's England, whatever the actual scope of women's activities, home was held to be the woman's place: the *domus*, from which [the] word domestic is derived, a private dwelling set in opposition to the public forum of politics.... Portia's suspicions echo Brutus's earlier admission that killing Caesar seems 'a dreadful thing', [yet] her appearance privatizes and more importantly, feminizes his hesitation. In terms of 'the general good' as Brutus's republicanism defines it, individual moral scruples must be overcome; if such scruples are associated with a woman, and voiced only in the home, all the more reason to disregard them. An opposition between private scruples and public action, however, does parallel an opposition between feminine fear and masculine constancy. It is such distinctions that underpin the construction of Brutus as a tragic hero who, though he entertains moral strictures against killing that are associated with the feminine and the private, must embrace a man's duty and repress them in the name of defending an abstract concept of the public weal.
>
> (Kahn, p. 99)

The public arena of politics in Rome is defined as male. Portia can only persuade Brutus to share his political secret by demonstrating male 'constancy' through wounding herself. But the fact of her femaleness allows Brutus to be absolved, as it were, of his fears and doubts because they are socially constructed as 'feminine'. And in the wider picture, Kahn draws attention to the society as gendered: all the male characters operating within a political ethos that has inscribed itself as narrowly 'masculine'.

Theatrical criticism

Thomas Platter and Leonard Digges are the earliest known critics of *Julius Caesar*, and criticism of performance has existed throughout the play's subsequent stage life, reflecting not just the current literary opinion of the day, but also responding to the interpretation and interaction of actors – what we might call their creative criticism. Latterly that creative criticism has extended to designers, directors, and a wide range of technical and production staff. Although in the nineteenth century a number of critics condemned stage performance as not living up to the experience of reading Shakespeare, the twentieth century came to see value in investigating the plays as, for us as for Shakespeare, scripts to be realized collaboratively in performance.

The most substantial survey is John Ripley's *Julius Caesar on Stage in England and America, 1599–1973*. Each major production is analysed in terms of the acting text, stagecraft, and acting, with a wide range of critical and contextual detail to reveal the significance of decisions made in preparing and presenting the play. Ripley quotes revealingly from practitioners, as when he notes Beerbohm Tree's comment, 'For the scholar Brutus, for the actor Cassius, for the public Antony' (Ripley, p. 151).

The modern confluence of literary with theatrical criticism might be dated from the publication of Harley Granville-Barker's *Prefaces to Shakespeare* from the late 1920s. Granville-Barker was a remarkable theatre director who had radicalized Shakespearean production, and whose Prefaces combine theatrical wisdom with an astute sensibility and a new historical knowledge of Elizabethan theatre. He is often at his best with detail; for instance, noting how the tears of Octavius' servant when he enters at the end of III.i can serve to fire Antony's imagination about the potential to move his hearers at Caesar's funeral, Granville-Barker inveighs against the stupidity of ending the scene early, after 'carrion men, groaning for burial' (III.i.275):

> How many modern actors upon their picture stage, with its curtain to close a scene for them pat upon some triumphant top note, have brought this one to its end twenty lines earlier [i.e. with the entire servant episode, ll. 276–97, cut]. . . . But to how untimely an end! The mechanism of Shakespeare's theater forbade such effects. Caesar's body is lying on the main stage, and must be removed, and it will take at least two people to carry it. . . . But as ever with Shakespeare, and with any artist worth his salt, limitation is turned to advantage. If dead Caesar is to be the mainspring of the play's further action, what more forceful way could be found of making this plain than, for a finish to the scene, to state the new theme of Octavius' coming, Caesar's kin and successor?
>
> (Granville-Barker, p. 369, fn.6)

A number of more recent scholars have developed our sense of how valuable it is to understand the theatrical as well as the literary modes and structures of the play, and how the live act of the performance needs as much analysis as the text. John Russell Brown has been at the forefront of this criticism since his landmark book *Shakespeare's Plays in Performance* in 1966, which includes a few examples from *Julius Caesar* that amply illustrate how an actor's motivation, interpretation, voice, stage movement, and especially understanding of subtext will affect audience response. In a subsequent essay devoted to *Julius Caesar*, Brown works in great detail with the stage effect of metre, interrupted lines, the orchestration of voices. He describes how, in the moments after Caesar's death, the stage action may be eloquent:

> [T]he stage is alive with action and cries. . . . At this point Shakespeare contrasts the isolated figure of Publius. Brutus first calls for him, and probably a pause follows as he is searched out, for the verse-line (85) is not completed. When he is found the audience, with the [conspirators], will turn attention on this aged senator. He is unmoving and silent, 'quite confounded'. Metellus seems to catch fear from him. . . . Shakespeare holds the dramatic focus on this paralysed figure still longer, as Cassius tries to get him to leave for the sake of his own safety, and Brutus briefly follows suit. . . . Everything has been held back by the panic-stricken Publius, with whom the conspirators are powerless, as he with them. Shakespeare has made a physical detail dominate the stage and provide an exposure of isolation, helplessness and fear.
>
> (Brown, pp. 120–1)

This example indicates the tendency for theatrical criticism to deal with the play as it unfolds, moment by moment, just as the commentary in Chapter 2 of this book does. Only through accumulation of these performance details, as experienced by an audience, can we move to a critical overview of the play.

M. M. Mahood gives a useful example of how attention to detail may reveal a theatrical pattern that throws new light on the play. Expanding on what Brown did with Publius, she concentrates on all the minor characters in *Julius Caesar*:

> Only within the lifetime of my own generation have Shakespeare's Titinius and his death been restored to the play in performance. His disappearance for over two hundred years was only one of the ways in which the actor-managers distorted *Julius Caesar* by eliminating between ten and eighteen of its minor characters. . . . Upward of a dozen minimal characters [are, in the second half of the play] pressed into the playwright's service to help us to experience the devotion which Brutus, with all his faults and with none

of Antony's charisma, is able to inspire ... they transform the mood of the play.... Two members of this small fraternity in defeat, Clitus and Dardanius, sustain the impression given by other minor characters that when Brutus's companions fall there are numbers more to replace them at his side... Strato is the last of the minor characters whom Shakespeare conjures into life from Plutarch's brief mention of them in order to concentrate our emotions, in this second part of the play, upon the tragedy of Brutus.

(Mahood, pp. 114–32)

There are a number of books that collect not only critical responses to the play in performance, but also increasingly publications from actors and directors on their own experience of Shakespeare on stage and on screen. But, as Brown warns, we need to be alert to the fact that each presentation will be different:

As the audience changes and encourages the actors in differing ways, so performance changes. A small stage accentuates different qualities in a text from those revealed on a large stage; a cold auditorium gives its own basic rhythm; the topical political climate will give particular emphasis to certain words; the physical weight of an actor will make the rhythms and proportions of his performance unique, and so will his emotional make-up and intellectual history. When Shakespeare decided to write for the theatre, he chose a medium that is adventitious: its effects are always being modified by interpreters and context.

(Brown, p. 131)

Further Reading

I The text and early performances

(i) Editions

Reliable one-volume editions of the play, with scholarly introductions, annotations and textual collations, include those by David Daniell (Arden Shakespeare, Third Series; Walton-on-Thames: Nelson, 1998); Marvin Spevack (New Cambridge Shakespeare; Cambridge: Cambridge University Press, 1988); and Arthur Humphreys (Oxford Shakespeare; Oxford and New York: Oxford University Press, 1984). Quotations and references in this *Handbook* are taken from the Humphreys edition.

(ii) Theatre history and theatre practice

Authority for the factual information in Chapter 1 will be found in the following books and in the editions cited above.

Andrew Gurr, *The Shakespearean Stage*, 3rd edn (Cambridge: Cambridge University Press, 1992). A thoroughly responsible account of what is known about the theatrical conditions in which Shakespeare's plays were first performed.

Jean MacIntyre, *Costumes and Scripts in the Elizabethan Theatres* (Edmonton: University of Alberta Press, 1992). A detailed analysis of the evidence from the theatres and the Office of the Revels about how costumes were used on the stage.

II General studies

Adrien Bonjour, *The Structure of Julius Caesar* (Liverpool: Liverpool University Press, 1958). A compact introduction to the play with special emphasis on its antithetical, and therefore ambivalent, structure.

John Russell Brown, *Shakespeare's Dramatic Style* (London: Heinemann, 1970). Covers a number of plays, has a chapter on *Julius Caesar* that demonstrates the value of alert close reading with an eye to performative qualities.

David Daiches, *Shakespeare: Julius Caesar* (London: Edward Arnold, 1976). A concise introductory reading of the play.

Leonard F. Dean (ed.), *Twentieth Century Interpretations of Julius Caesar: A Collection of Critical Essays* (Englewood Cliffs, NJ: Prentice-Hall, 1968). A casebook that usefully assembles a number of significant articles on the play.

Vivian Thomas, *Julius Caesar* (Hemel Hempstead: Harvester Wheatsheaf, 1992). Provides an overview of the play with useful attention to the critical reception.

Peter Ure (ed.), *Julius Caesar: A Casebook* (London: Macmillan, 1969). A casebook that not only reprints influential articles, but also a brief selection of pre-twentieth-century criticism.

Richard Wilson (ed.), *Julius Caesar*, New Casebooks (Basingstoke: Palgrave Macmillan, 2002). A casebook that reprints significant essays reflecting the application of the new critical theory of recent years.

III   Sources

Geoffrey Bullough (ed.), *Narrative and Dramatic Sources of Shakespeare*, vol 5 (London and New York: Routledge and Kegan Paul and Columbia University Press, 1964). Contains not only the selections from North's Plutarch that Shakespeare certainly used, but also many other possible sources.

Christian Meier, *Caesar*, trans. David McLintock (New York: Basic Books, 1996). A thoughtful standard biography of Julius Caesar.

James Shapiro, *1599: A Year in the Life of William Shakespeare* (London: Faber and Faber, 2005). A biographical account of the events of 1599 as valuable source material for understanding Shakepeare's social context at the time.

T. J. B. Spencer (ed.), *Shakespeare's Plutarch* (Harmondsworth: Penguin, 1964). An accessible volume of the Plutarch sections used by Shakespeare with the related passages from the play usefully printed on the same page.

IV   The play in production and performance

Ralph Berry, *On Directing Shakespeare* (London and New York: Croom Helm/Barnes and Noble, 1977). Interviews with seven leading stage

directors, including forceful comments from three on their productions of *Julius Caesar*.

B. S. Field, *Shakespeare's Julius Caesar: A Production Collection* (Chicago:
Nelson-Hall, 1980). A collection of photos from seven productions,
with commentary from their actors and directors.

Peter Holland, *English Shakespeares: Shakespeare on the English Stage in the
1990s* (Cambridge: Cambridge University Press, 1997). A lively collection of reviews, including David Thacker's 1993 RSC production
of *Julius Caesar* and others.

John Ripley, *Julius Caesar on Stage in England and America, 1599–1973*
(Cambridge: Cambridge University Press, 1980). Too full of detail to
be easily readable, but hugely valuable for reference and individual
productions.

Gāmini Salgādo (ed.), *Eyewitnesses of Shakespeare: First Hand Accounts of
Performances 1590–1890* (London: Sussex University Press/Chatto
and Windus, 1975). A useful compilation of pre-twentieth-century
critical responses.

Arthur Colby Sprague, *Shakespeare and the Actors* (Cambridge, MA:
Harvard University Press, 1948). An often entertaining collection of
particular bits of actor interpretation or business, including *Julius
Caesar*.

Reviews of British productions since 1981 are collected and republished
in the periodical *Theatre Record*.

V   Screen and audio versions

Because recordings are liable to be offered in varying formats with new
reference numbers, only titles and directors' names are given here
together with the original release date; from this information, the
latest and most convenient reissue can be identified.

(i) Screen versions described in this Handbook

Julius Caesar, directed by David Bradley, 1950.
Julius Caesar, directed by Joseph L. Mankiewicz, 1953.
Julius Caesar, directed by Stuart Burge, 1970.
Julius Caesar, directed by Herbert Wise, 1979 (BBC Shakespeare).
A complete listing of all screen productions is given in Rothwell's
History of Shakespeare on Screen (see below).

(ii) Audio versions

Julius Caesar, directed by George Rylands, with members of the Marlowe Society and professional actors (Argo, 1958).

Julius Caesar, directed by Howard Sackler (Caedmon, 1964; now HarperCollins).

Julius Caesar, directed by Clive Brill (Arkangel, 2003).

Julius Caesar, directed by Orson Welles (Pavilion/Pearl).

(iii) Books on screen versions

John Houseman, *Front and Center* (New York: Simon and Schuster, 1979). An autobiography that includes discussion of production and artistic decisions surrounding the 1953 Mankiewicz film. See also *Run-through* under 'Critical assessments' below.

Kenneth Rothwell, *A History of Shakespeare on Screen*, 2nd edn. (Cambridge: Cambridge University Press, 2004). Includes a list of all films of *Julius Caesar*, and lively if somewhat opinionated criticism of the major films.

John Wilders (ed.), *Julius Caesar*, BBC TV Shakespeare (London: BBC, 1979). This edition of the play includes cuts and changes to the text made in the BBC television shooting script, and useful brief essays on intentions and process.

VI   Critical assessments

Catherine Belsey, *The Subject of Tragedy* (London and New York: Methuen, 1985).

A. C. Bradley, *Shakespearean Tragedy* (London: Macmillan, 1957 [first pub. 1904]).

Sigurd Burckhardt, 'How Not to Murder Caesar', in *Shakespearean Meanings* (Princeton, NJ: Princeton University Press, 1968).

Ian Donaldson, '"Misconstruing Everything": *Julius Caesar* and *Sejanus*', in *Shakespeare Performed: Essays in Honor of R. A. Foakes*, ed. Grace Ioppolo (Newark, DE and London: University of Delaware Press/ Associated University Presses, 2000).

Harley Granville-Barker, 'Julius Caesar', in *Prefaces to Shakespeare*, vol. 2 (London: Batsford, 1958).

William Hazlitt, 'Julius Caesar', in *The Round Table and Characters of Shakespear's Plays*, ed. Catherine Macdonald Maclean (London: Dent, 1936).

Lisa Hopkins, *The Cultural Uses of the Caesars on the English Renaissance Stage* (Aldershot and Burlington, VT: Ashgate, 2008).

John Houseman, *Run-through* (New York: Simon and Schuster, 1980). See also *Front and Center* under 'Books on screen versions'.

Coppélia Kahn, *Roman Shakespeare: Warriors, Wounds, and Women* (London and New York: Routledge, 1997).

Paulina Kewes, 'Julius Caesar in Jacobean England', *The Seventeenth Century* 17 (2000), pp. 155–86.

G. Wilson Knight, *The Wheel of Fire*, (London: Oxford University Press and Humphrey Milford, 1930).

G. Wilson Knight, *The Imperial Theme*, 3rd edn. (London: Methuen, 1951).

M. W. MacCallum, *Shakespeare's Roman Plays* (London: Macmillan, 1910).

M. M. Mahood, *Playing Bit Parts in Shakespeare* (London and New York: Routledge, 1998 [first published as *Bit Parts in Shakespeare's Plays* by Cambridge University Press in 1992]).

Geoffrey Miles, *Shakespeare and the Constant Romans* (Oxford: Clarendon Press, 1996).

Robert S. Miola, *Shakespeare's Rome* (Cambridge: Cambridge University Press, 1983).

Robert S. Miola, 'Julius Caesar and the Tyrannicide Debate', *Renaissance Quarterly* 38, 2 (Summer 1985), pp. 271–89.

Gail Kern Paster, '"In the spirit of men there is no blood": Blood as Trope of Gender in *Julius Caesar*', *Shakespeare Quarterly* 40 (1989), pp. 248–98.

Clifford Ronan, *'Anticke Roman': Power, Symbology and the Roman Play in Early Modern England, 1585–1635* (Athens, GA and London: University of Georgia Press, 1995).

Ernest Schanzer, *The Problem Plays of Shakespeare* (London: Routledge and Kegan Paul, 1963).

Steve Sohmer, *Shakespeare's Mystery Play: The Opening of the Globe Theatre, 1599* (Manchester and New York: Manchester University Press, 1999).

T. J. B. Spencer, 'Shakespeare and the Elizabethan Romans', *Shakespeare Survey* 10 (1957), pp. 27–38.

Caroline Spurgeon, *Shakespeare's Imagery* (Cambridge: Cambridge University Press, 1935).

J. Dover Wilson (ed.), *Julius Caesar* (Cambridge: Cambridge University Press, 1949).

Richard Wilson, 'Is This a Holiday?', in *Will Power: Essays on Shakespearean Authority* (Detroit: Wayne State University Press, 1993).

Index